THE
NOW
PROPHECIES

DISASTER IN IRAN
DESTRUCTION OF DAMASCUS
DECLINE OF AMERICA
THE FINAL ARAB-ISRAELI WAR

BILL SALUS

W9-CLC-203

First printing February 2016
Printed in the United States of America

Copyright ©2016 by Bill Salus. All rights reserved. This book or parts thereof may not be reproduced in any form, stored in a retrieval system, or transmitted in any form by any means - electronic, mechanical, photocopy, recording, or otherwise - without prior written permission of the publisher, except as provided by United States of America copyright law.

Published in the United States

Prophecy Depot Publishing

Books are available in quantity for promotional or premium use.

For information contact:

Prophecy Depot Ministries
P.O. Box 5612
La Quinta, CA 92248

Design Director: Matthew Curtis Salhus

Image Designer: Lani Harmony Salhus

ISBN – 978-0-9887260-7-9

All Bible verses are taken from the New King James Version unless otherwise notated.

Please visit our website for other Prophecy Depot Ministries products:
http://www.prophecydepot.com

Acknowledgements

Heartfelt thanks to my wife, children, and grandchildren who inspired me to write this book. A further debt of gratitude is extended to all those who in one way or another, through prayer, encouragement, support, research, or otherwise, genuinely blessed this book.

This book is dedicated to the one true loving God of the Bible; the Holy One in Israel!

So I will make My holy name known in the midst of My people Israel, and I will not let them profane My holy name anymore. Then the nations shall know that I am the LORD, the Holy One in Israel. Surely it is coming, and it shall be done," says the Lord GOD. "This is the day of which I have spoken.

— Ezekiel 39:7-8

Table of Contents

Appendices

Introducing The NOW Prophecies

It was 1:59 a.m. on the early morning of Friday, October 16, 2015, when I was awoken from a dream by a phone call. It was an unfamiliar phone number from an overseas country. I initially thought it was my phone alarm ringing, which had been set for 6:30 a.m. to take my grandchildren to school that morning. This was going to be a special occasion as my wife and I were visiting them on vacation.

As I reached over to turn the alarm off, I noticed that it was pitch black out and something wasn't right. When I looked at my phone I saw an unidentified number and thought to myself, "This isn't my alarm, this is a strange phone number. Who could be calling me at this early hour?" In the few minutes that followed, I questioned if, "The unusual timing and unknown origin of the call was providential rather than coincidental." Introspectively, I wondered, "Did the Lord just wake me up on purpose?"

This reasoning might strike you as odd, considering the fact that I was awoken from a dead sleep and my mental faculties were far from functioning. I mean, It was dark out and I hadn't even ingested my first cup of coffee, which essentially means, I'm operating in do not disturb mode!

However, it was the dream that got me thinking this way. It provided me with the impetus to get up, rather than sleep in until the alarm would go off at 6:30 a.m. I recognized that if I went back to sleep I would probably forget the details within the dream. So I got up to pray about the dream.

I even saved the phone number from the mysterious caller and a few days later returned the call, but guess what? It was a wrong number belonging to someone, somewhere in Africa who doesn't speak a word of English. Did man's mistake equal God's providence in this matter?[1] I believe that the errant phone call served as an important wake up alert to get me working on the NOW Prophecies project.

In the dream, I was aware that the Lord was speaking to me. The message He gave me was simply, "I want you to name your next work, *The NOW Prophecies*!" I had spent a good part of 2015 preparing some new teaching messages, and the focus was on preparing for the prophecies that appear ready to find their fulfillment. Thus, this title was perfect, a godsend.

"That's it," I said to myself inside the dream. "That's what the Lord wants me to do. He has given me the perfect name for my next project." Still dreaming, I marveled in a blissful state about this inspired message. A few minutes into my bliss the phone rang, and all of the above occurred.

Immediately after dropping the grandkids off at school that day I began writing "*The NOW Prophecies*." The words flowed from my fingers to the keyboard like a fountain overflowing with water. The culmination of my years of research was being encapsulated into an easy to understand book and DVD that would be made available for the average American household.

The debates about the accuracy of my discernments of the NOW Prophecies have already been published in my prior works. They are available for any reader that wants to achieve a deeper understanding about these prophecies. Therefore, I'm not going to reprove what has previously been proven, nor rehash the arguments that I have already addressed. This project is not intended to improve upon what was previously revealed, but rather it exists to inform the masses about the coming globally impacting events; the prophecies that this generation needs to prepare for. The ancient predictions that are going to happen NOW!

CAVEAT: The title and the concept of this book were inspired by my dream. However, the details and the content were the product of biblical research combined with prayer and circumstantial confirmations. Whether or not this is a Holy Spirit inspired work will be for you to discern. I sincerely believe that this book will provide you with the invaluable information that you need to know NOW!

What are the NOW Prophecies?

Millions of books adorn bookshelves worldwide, with all sorts of information about the past and the future, but the NOW Prophecies deal with the most relevant information for this present age. This is because they describe events that will likely find fulfillment during this generation's existence. All unfulfilled biblical prophecy is important to understand, but of most value to any given group, past, present or future, is the information that was specifically provided through the ancient Hebrew prophecies for that generation's benefit.

The NOW Prophecies are the unfulfilled ancient biblical predictions that appear to be imminent, which means they could happen NOW! These foretellings have either minor or no remaining preconditions inhibiting them from happening.

Noah was given a NOW Prophecy about a forthcoming worldwide flood. Joseph's NOW Prophecies dealt with seven years of plenty that would be swallowed up by seven years of ensuing famine in Egypt. The prophet Jeremiah warned about seventy years of desolation in Judah and the corresponding Jewish dispersion from Judah during those years.

In all of these instances it was the NOW Prophecies that benefited the affected populations the most. These timely predictions enabled the peoples of those times to prepare for the powerful events that directly affected them! Likewise, you need to know the predictions that could affect you NOW!

Which are the NOW Prophecies?

The NOW Prophecies include, but are not limited to, the following globally impacting events. They are the;

- Disaster in Iran – (Jeremiah 49:34-39),
- Destruction of Damascus – (Isaiah 17, Jer. 49:23-27),
- Toppling of Jordan – (Jer. 49:1-6, Zephaniah 2:8-10, Ezekiel 25:14),
- Terrorization of Egypt – (Isaiah 19:1-18),
- Final Arab-Israeli War- (Psalm 83),
- Decline of America (Ezekiel 38:13), (*America is identified as the young lions of Tarshish*)
- Expansion of Israel – (Obadiah 1:19-20, Jer. 49:2, Zephaniah 2:9, Isaiah 19:18),
- Vanishing of the Christians – (1 Corinthians 15:51-52, 1 Thessalonians 4:15-18).

NOW, NEXT and LAST Prophecies

There are three categories of coming biblical prophecies. They are the;

1. **NOW Prophecies,**
2. **NEXT Prophecies,**
3. **LAST Prophecies.**

The *NEXT Prophecies* are those that follow the fulfillment of the NOW Prophecies. In essence, the NOW's provide the necessary nexus of events that pave the path for the execution of the NEXT Prophecies. Although the NEXT Prophecies are rapidly racing toward fulfillment, they require the completion of the NOW's in order for their stage to become appropriately set.

The *LAST Prophecies* still have significant preconditions preventing them from finding fulfillment. They will find fulfillment relatively soon, but the LAST's have to wait in line behind the NOW's and NEXT's for their turn on the prophetic timeline.

When will the NOW Prophecies happen?

This book explains that NOW spans the period of time existing between the establishment of the Jewish state of Israel, which happened in 1948, and the fulfillment of the Ezekiel 38 and 39 prophecies. NOW is where mankind is presently situated on the prophetic timeline. We exist between these two marquee events.

The Ezekiel 38 and 39 foretellings are epic events. Through these prophecies, the Lord intends to notify the world that He is the one true God! This important notification from the Lord is the underlying theme within this book.

These Ezekiel events appear to be coming soon, but due to the outstanding preconditions described in Ezekiel 38:7-13, these predictions should not be categorized as NOW prophecies. They are better classified as NEXT prophecies. The preconditions in Ezekiel 38:7-13 will be removed, only after certain NOW prophecies conclude. This is why it is important to determine what the NOW prophecies entail, because their fulfillment segues into Ezekiel 38 and 39.

If the Ezekiel 38 and 39 experiences are about to happen, then the NOW prophecies that precede them, must find their fulfillment very soon! Only the Lord knows when these NOW prophecies will occur, but all present indications suggest that they should happen during this present generation. God is gracious, merciful and extremely long-suffering, which means that the timing of the NOW prophecies are ultimately up to Him.

We don't know when the Lord will give the green light on the NOW prophecies, but we do know the details of the predictions. Therefore, it is easier to determine the sequence of the NOW prophecies than their precise timing.

Since the NOW Prophecies do not appear to happen at the exact same time, I sequenced them above in the order that I believe they could likely occur. Placing these predictions in their correct chronological order is, at best, an educated guess. However, the fact that these predictions are in the NOW category implies that only a minimal amount of time lapses between each event. One NOW episode should trigger the next one to follow relatively promptly on its heels.

The birth pain analogy applies in the sequencing of these NOW events. Likened to a woman about to become a mother through the birthing of her child, the NOW's initiate the process of events leading to the return of Jesus Christ at His Second Coming!

As the baby descends down the birth canal, the mother's contractions become more intense, more frequent, and unstoppable! Similarly, once the NOW Prophecies begin they become more extreme, recurrent and unpreventable!

Why are the NOW Prophecies happening?

The fulfillment of the NOW Prophecies accomplishes specific purposes within the prophetic plans of God. The end of each episode evidences that the will of the Lord was manifested within and throughout the epic event.

For instance, Psalm 83 results in the end of the ancient Arab hatred of the Jews described in Ezekiel 35:5 and 25:15. It also proves that the Lord's Gentile foreign policy inscribed in Genesis 12:3 remains effectually intact. This is demonstrated by the cursing of the Psalm 83 Arabs for wanting to curse Israel in the prophetic war. Genesis 12:3 vows a curse upon those that would curse Israel. Several other Scriptures show that this pronouncement to Abraham extends down through the genealogy of his son Isaac and his grandson Jacob, who in Genesis 32:28 was renamed Israel.

"I will bless those who bless you, (Abraham)
And I will curse him who curses you;
And in you all the families of the earth shall be blessed."

— Genesis 12:3; *emphasis added*

Summary

The Merriam –Webster dictionary defines the word now as;

- At the present time,
- In the next moment: very soon,
- In the present situation.

NOW is the time to prepare for the predicted events that are forthcoming. NOW is the time to get excited about what the Lord is preparing to do in the near future. The Creator of the universe is going to silence His critics, by utilizing His supernatural powers in order to demonstrate His supremacy over the earth. The Ezekiel 38 and 39 prophecies will provide the perfect format for the Lord to accomplish this.

A worldwide audience will witness an unprecedented military victory, which is humanly unexplainable, over a powerful nine member coalition led by Russia, which includes Turkey, and Iran. They will coalesce to conquer Israel, but the Lord will miraculously defend the survival of the modern day Jewish state. In the process, the nations of the world will be notified that the God of the Bible is the one and only true God of the universe. This is all explained in great detail in the prophecies of Ezekiel 38 and 39.

This book explores the events that happen between NOW and then. Best Reading Regards to all of you.

Where Are We NOW On God's Timeline?

The Prophetic Timeline

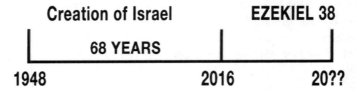

Creation of Israel   EZEKIEL 38

68 YEARS

1948   2016   20??

Before exploring the NOW Prophecies, it is important to discuss our present placement on God's calendar of events. Unquestionably, the most important prophetic information for every generation is the knowledge of its whereabouts on the Lord's prophetic timeline. The prophet Isaiah informs us that there exists a definite beginning and end, so the logical question is where are we NOW?

> "Remember the former things of old, For I *am* God, and *there is* no other; *I am* God, and *there is* none like Me, Declaring the end from the beginning, And from ancient times *things* that are not *yet* done, Saying, 'My counsel shall stand, And I will do all My pleasure."
>
> — Isaiah 46:9-10

The simple answer is that we are somewhere between the two prophetic events of the rebirth of the nation Israel and the Ezekiel

39:7 upholding of the Lord's holy name through the nation of Israel. In fulfillment of numerous prophecies, Israel was reborn as a nation on May 14, 1948. This is when the end time's hourglass made its final turn, and now the grains of sand are rapidly descending downward into its lower chamber. Mankind is racing toward the expiration date of this present earth.

These two marquee events should standout like monumental bookends to this generation because they are intended to serve as the prophetic proof that the God of the Bible is the one true God over all the earth. Replacement theology, the erroneous teaching that God's done with the Jews, has facilitated the failure of many Christians to recognize the miraculous existence of the Jewish state of Israel. However, their ignorance does not erase the fact that Israel today is a marvelous sovereign undertaking of the Lord. According to the prophet Jeremiah it was intended to be so.

> "Therefore, behold, *the* days are coming," says the LORD, "that they shall no longer say, 'As the LORD lives who brought up the children of Israel from the land of Egypt,' but, 'As the LORD lives who brought up and led the descendants of the house of Israel from the north country and from all the countries where I had driven them.' And they shall dwell in their own land."
>
> — Jeremiah 23:7-8

The Hebrew exodus from Egypt resulted in the parting of the Red Sea (Exodus 14). This was a supernatural event that has yet to be outmatched or duplicated to this day. This miracle was to be memorialized in the minds of the Hebrew generations that followed. It served to remind the Jews that their God Jehovah could deliver them through all obstacles and oppressions. In addition to this monumental miracle, the Old Testament is filled with other historical examples evidencing this fact.

However, Jeremiah 23:7 declares that the exodus episode will pale in comparison to the modern day miracle of the rebirthed nation of Israel. Rightfully so, the Lord had to accomplish much more than parting the Red Sea in order to reestablish the nation of Israel in modernity. Below are a few examples depicting the enormous sovereign undertaking of God in order for Israel to exist today!

- *Implant Zionism in Jews* – Zionism is the term associated with the national movement for the return of the Jewish people to their homeland and the resumption of Jewish sovereignty in the Land of Israel.[2] In the late 1800's, after centuries of existence outside of their country, the Jews began to yearn to return back to their ancient homeland. They were, and still are, willing to leave their world countries, diverse cultures and differing languages to return to a place that was desolate and is presently dangerous.

- *Create Arab Homelands* – From 1517 – 1917 A.D. the Middle East was under the control of the Ottoman Empire. The domination abruptly ended with the Turkish loss in World War I. This empire had to be eliminated in order for the Mideast to be rezoned with Arab states and a Jewish state. The creation of the Arab states and the Jewish state was the fulfillment of the Lord's Mideast Peace Plan provided in Jeremiah 12:14-17. The prophecy specified that the Arabs and Jews would return to their homelands, which occurred in the aftermath of the collapse of the Ottoman Empire.

"Thus says the LORD: "Against all My evil neighbors who touch the inheritance which I have caused My people Israel to inherit—behold, I will pluck them out of their land and pluck out the house of Judah from among them. Then it shall be, after I have plucked them out, that I will return and have compassion on them and bring them back, everyone (Jews and Arabs) to his heritage and everyone to his land. And it shall be, if they will learn carefully the ways of My people, to swear by My name, 'As the LORD lives,' as they taught My people to swear by Baal, then they shall be established in the midst of My people. But if they do not obey, I will utterly pluck up and destroy that nation," says the LORD."

— Jeremiah 12:14-17; *emphasis added*

Afghanistan	1919
Egypt	1922
Saudi Arabia & Iraq	1932
Iran	1935
Lebanon	1943
Syria & Jordan	1946
Israel	1948

It's important to note that Jeremiah 12:17 predicts the destruction of the Arab nations that curse Israel instead of live peacefully alongside Israel. This destruction seemingly occurs with the NOW prophecy of Psalm 83.

- *Prevent Nazi Genocide* – In order for the Jewish state to exist, Jews needed to exist. During World War II, Adolph Hitler and the Nazis attempted the genocide of the Jews. Had they been successful, there would be no Israel today! Whereas, World War I freed up the ancient land of Israel for the Jewish people. World War II prepared the Jews for the land of Israel.

- *Empower the Allied Forces* – Communist Russia teamed up with the capitalistic America and the other allied forces to defeat the Nazis. This cohesion of this unlikely coalition was also the miraculous sovereign undertaking of the Lord.

- *Create the Jewish State* – With the control of the Otto-
man Empire relinquished and the establishment of the
Arab states in place, the restoration of Israel occurred.
These territorial shifts paved the way for the state of
Israel to come into existence.

- *Empower the Israeli Army* – Ezekiel 37:10, 25:14, Obadiah 1:18 and elsewhere predicted the rise of today's Israeli
Defense Forces (IDF). Through the process of three
regional wars in 1948, 1967 and 1973, the Jews trans-
formed from refugees into the most powerful army in
the Middle East. This had to happen in order to sustain
Israel's existence.

- *Preserve and Prosper Israel* – Israel is becoming a prosperous nation. According to Ezekiel 38:12-13, Israel continues to prosper and achieve an abundance of plunder
and booty. It is this prosperity that motivates the Russian
Gog of Magog invaders to attack Israel.

The Upholding of God's Holy Name through His People Israel

The Magog invasion of Ezekiel 38-39 is the other major prophetic marker for this generation to consider. Ezekiel 38:1-39:20,
contains forty-three verses of some of the most consolidated and
descriptive prophetic information found anywhere within the entire Bible.

The reader of these passages doesn't need to be a bible scholar,
rocket scientist, or even a believer to glean a relatively detailed understanding of this forthcoming prophecy. By interpreting these
verses literally the reader is made aware of the:

- *Timing of the event* – (In the end times), Ezek. 38:8, 16.
- *Identities of the invading coalition* – (Refer to the map for
a consensus of whom many scholars believe participates.

I call them the "Outer Ring" because they don't share common borders with Israel). Ezek. 38:1-5.

- *Motivation for the invasion of Israel* – (To take spoil, plunder and booty from Israel). Ezek. 38:12-13.
- *Conditions inside Israel at the time of the invasion* – (A nation at peace that is dwelling securely without walls). Ezek. 38:8, 11, 14.
- *Defeat of the invaders by supernatural means* - (Earthquake, pestilence, bloodshed, flooding rains, great hailstones, fire and brimstone). Ezek. 38:18-23.
- *Aftermath of the event* – (Israel will gain international renown for burying the dead for seven months and burning the invaders weapons for seven years). Ezek. 39:9-16.
- *Purpose of the prophecy* – (The upholding of the holy name of God). Ezek. 39:7.

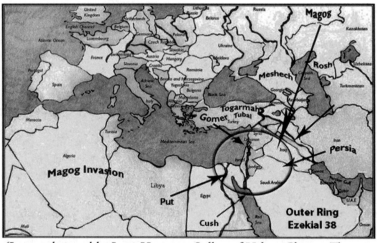

(Images designed by Lani Harmony Salhus of Urban Charm. They picture the ancient names superimposed over their modern day equivalents).

The Lord appears to have intended these verses to be relatively easy for everyone to understand, because this is the epic event through which He pledges to notify the world that He is the one true God!

There will be no way to misconstrue that the supernatural destruction of the Magog invaders came exclusively through the hand of the Lord. Although Israel is positively identified within this prophecy, and possibly even America, the victory over the Russian coalition will not be attributed to either, but the Lord will get the full credit. Let's say this: "In the aftermath, He alone will receive credit for Israel's victory. The Lord will have validated His sovereignty over the affairs of men as declared in Isaiah 46:10, "*I* (the Lord) *will do all My pleasure*".

The Lord will be able to proclaim, with absolute authority, that He is the covenant keeping God of Abraham, Isaac and Jacob, who sent his only begotten Son, Jesus Christ, so that all who receive Him as their Lord and Savior would not perish but have eternal life.

In the chapter entitled, "Ezekiel 38: The Israeli Perspective," I provide a brief commentary of the Gog of Magog war. This chapter addresses my views on the timing of this prophecy, which I believe occurs before the seven year Tribulation Period commences, (*i.e.* Daniel's Seventieth Week). It also explores why the Rapture probably occurs before both Ezekiel 38 and the Tribulation Period.

In the chapter called, "The Decline of America," biblical, historical and geo-political arguments are provided, which evidence how America could be identified in Ezekiel 38:13, as the young lions of the merchants of Tarshish. America in this prophecy is depicted as a lesser nation, a meager sideline spectator of the Magog invasion. America, shrunken to this non-superpower stature, appears to occur as one of the NOW Prophecies.

The Gap Between The NOW And NEXT Prophecies

(What's in the gap?)

Creation of Israel		EZEKIEL 38
68 YEARS		Gap?
1948	2016	20??

As important as the NEXT prophecies described in Ezekiel 38-39 are, they do not appear ready to happen now. There exists a gap between now and then. The following section explains how this conclusion can be drawn.

Ezekiel 38:7-13 lists several prerequisites that must exist inside of Israel before the Magog invasion can occur. Israel must be a reestablished nation in the latter years, which is the case today. However, the country needs to be inhabited by a peaceful Jewish people that dwell securely without walls, bars or gates. Additionally, Israel must possess a sufficient surplus of spoils, because that is what the Magog coalition comes after.

If this prophecy is to be interpreted literally, it is safe to say that Israel is not dwelling without walls. In fact, the Middle East is the most fenced in and fortified region in the world and Israel is arguably the most walled in country in the entire Mideast.

Some contend that Israel is dwelling securely today. They generally define the security described in Ezekiel 38: 8, 11, and 14, as a relative confidence in the ability of the IDF to defend the Jewish nation. Although I agree that the IDF can defend Israel today, I thoroughly disagree with this interpretation. Ezekiel's intended usage of the Hebrew words for dwelling securely, deals with a security that is achieved through military conquest over Israel's surrounding Arab enemies. We discover this ten chapters earlier in Ezekiel 28.

> "And there shall no longer be a pricking brier or a painful thorn for the house of Israel from among all *who are* around them, who despise them. Then they shall know that I *am* the Lord GOD." "Thus says the Lord GOD: "When I have gathered the house of Israel from the peoples among whom they are scattered, and am hallowed in them in the sight of the Gentiles, then they will dwell in their own land which I gave to My servant Jacob. And they will dwell safely there, build houses, and plant vineyards; yes, they will dwell securely, when I execute judgments on all those around them who despise them. Then they shall know that I *am* the LORD their God.""

— Ezekiel 28:24-26

The pertinent question for today is; "Does Israel have enemies surrounding them that despise them?" The answer to that question is definitely YES! They all happen to be enlisted in the ancient prophecy of Psalm 83. They comprise an inner circle of Arab states, and terrorist populations within those states, that share common borders with Israel. An overview of Psalm 83 is provided in the chapter called, "Psalm 83: The Final Arab-Israeli War."

Due to the existence of these unsatisfied prerequisite conditions spelled out in Ezekiel 38:7-13, the Ezekiel 38-39 predictions are appropriately classified as NEXT, but not NOW, prophecies.

This presumably precludes that at least Psalm 83, the concluding Arab-Israeli war, needs to happen before Israel can dwell securely and remove the walls that protect it from its surrounding enemies.

Thus, between now and the NEXT prophecies of Ezekiel 38, we can insert Psalm 83 as a stage setter for the Ezekiel events. Psalm 83 could happen at any time. The only minor conditions standing between now and Psalm 83 are two paper-thin peace treaties between Israel and Jordan and Israel and Egypt. Egypt, probably, and Jordan, certainly, are participants in Psalm 83.

What Prophecies fill the Gap between NOW and the Magog Invasion?

Psalm 83 is among the NOW prophecies that happen between now and the time that the Lord upholds His holy name in the Magog event. However, there are several other biblical predictions that could possibly happen before Ezekiel 38-39. This is a sobering potential reality if you consider the likelihood that Ezekiel 38 could happen within the next decade or so. I'm not predicting the timing of Ezekiel 38, but many of today's top scholars believe that the stage is set for Ezekiel 38 to happen very soon.

Although the Bible doesn't give us a specific date for the commencement point of Ezekiel 38-39, we are currently over six decades closer than we were in 1948 when Israel was rebirthed as the Jewish state. The question is, are we another sixty or more years until the Magog Invasion? I don't think so!

The NOW prophecies previously identified should all find fulfillment before the Lord upholds His holy name through His people Israel. The possible exception would be the vanishing of the Christians, (i.e. the Rapture of the Church). The timing of the Rapture could be before, during or after the Ezekiel 38-39 prophecies find fulfillment. The Rapture is explained in the chapter entitled, "The Vanishing of the Christians."

The Nuclear NOW Prophecy Of IRAN

Revealing the Ancient Prophecy of Elam

Disaster in Iran
(Elam Prophecy)

Creation of Israel		EZEKIEL 38
	68 YEARS	Jeremiah 49:34-39
1948	2016	20??

A t the top of my timing list for the NOW predictions is Jeremiah 49:34-39. This prophecy, authored around 596 B.C., seems to deal with what is presently taking place inside of Iran. This ancient foretelling breaks down into two parts, both of which are occurring NOW!

Jeremiah 49:34-37 appears to be alluding to Iran's military matters, specifically its nuclear and Intercontinental Ballistic Missiles (ICBM's) programs. Jeremiah 49:38-39 then shifts topics to the religious element and the burgeoning conflict between Islam and Christianity. Presently, Iran is producing the fastest growing evangelical Christian population per capita in the world. Christianity is growing at the pace of 19.6% per year in Iran.[3]

Rank	Country	Ann Gr*
1	Iran	19.6%
2	Afghanistan	16.7%
3	Gambia, The	8.9%
4	Cambodia	8.8%
5	Greenland	8.4%
6	Algeria	8.1%
7	Somalia	8.1%
8	Mongolia	7.9%
9	Kuwait	7.3%
10	Tajikistan	6.9%
11	Laos	6.8%
12	Mauritania	6.7%
13	Sao Tome & Principe	6.5%
14	Sudan	6.4%

Both of these topics are explored exhaustively in my book and accompanying DVD entitled, *Nuclear Showdown in Iran, Revealing the Ancient Prophecy of Elam.* The nuclear showdown primarily concerns Israel vs. Iran, and the spiritual showdown is between Islam and Christianity.

Seven times in the six verses of Jer. 49:34-39, the prophet says "*I will,*" alluding to what the Lord intends to accomplish concerning Elam. After each *I will* declaration follows an important *detail added* assertion that helps to clarify the extent of the predicted events. Connecting the *I wills'* with their corresponding *detail added assertions* is essential to understanding the specifics of the prophecy.

Before identifying these seven I wills, it is important to locate ancient Elam on a modern day map. Elam is the area of Iran that hugs the Persian Gulf. Elam represents about one-fifth of modern day Iran and Persia spreads across the remaining four-fifths of the nation. Persia was the name for Iran until 1935.

About 2700 years ago, two prophecies were issued about future judgments that would come upon Iran. Ezekiel 38:5 addressed Persia, and Jeremiah 49:34 concentrated on Elam. Notice on the map that Elam is the location of Iran's Bushehr nuclear reactor. It sits upon the convergence of three tectonic plates and is a nuclear disaster waiting to happen. In addition to this reactor, Iran has contracted with Russia to construct several more of these nuclear facilities in the same general area.

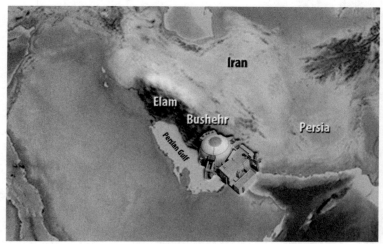

The text of Jeremiah 49:34-39

This section presents the text of Jeremiah 49:34-39 and identifies the seven I wills within the text. It is followed by a summary of the prophecies possible application for today.

"The word of the LORD that came to Jeremiah the prophet against Elam, in the beginning of the reign of

Zedekiah king of Judah, saying, "Thus says the
LORD of hosts: 'Behold, I will break the bow of
Elam, The foremost of their might. Against Elam I
will bring the four winds From the four quarters of
heaven, And scatter them toward all those winds; There
shall be no nations where the outcasts of Elam will not
go. For I will cause Elam to be dismayed before their
enemies And before those who seek their life. I will bring
disaster upon them, My fierce anger,' says the LORD;
'And I will send the sword after them Until I have
consumed them. I will set My throne in Elam, And will
destroy from there the king and the princes,' says the
LORD. 'But it shall come to pass in the latter days: I will
bring back the captives of Elam,' says the LORD."

— Jeremiah 49:34-39

The Seven I Wills of the Lord in Jeremiah 49:34-39

1. *The Lord will* break the bow of Elam. The detail added is,
    at the foremost of Elam's might. It is noteworthy to men-
    tion that Iran is presently at or approaching the pinnacle
    of its modern military and political might.

2. *The Lord will* gather the four winds from the four quar-
    ters of heaven. The detail is that these winds will scatter
    the affected population into all the nations of the world.
    This alludes to a worldwide dispersion.

3. *The Lord will* cause Iran to be dismayed. The detail is that
    this debilitating judgment will be witnessed, and probably
    caused, by Iran's enemies. The inference is that Iran will be
    humiliated and extremely beaten down, by its enemies.

4. *The Lord will* create a disaster inside Iran, specifically the
    territory of ancient Elam. The reason is because Iran has
    fiercely angered the Lord.

5. *The Lord will* send the sword after the Iranians. The detail is until they are defeated.

6. *The Lord will* destroy the Iranian leadership. The detail is that in the aftermath the Lord will establish His throne in Elam.

7. *The Lord will* restore the affected territory. The details are that this occurs in the latter days and alludes to the return and restoration of the dispersed Iranians, those that fled the area when the disaster occurred.

Summarizing the Elam prophecy

In this prophecy Jeremiah declares that a time would arrive when the Lord would be furious with the leadership of Iran. We know this because Jeremiah 49:38 says that the kings and the princes will be destroyed. This most likely represents the Iranian government in place when the prophecy occurs. The Lord would never destroy good kings and princes, so we can safely presume that bad Iranian leadership is the problem.

An example of good Iranian leadership was King Cyrus the Great of Persia who lived between 600-529 BC. Isaiah 44-45 predicted his arrival on the world scene a century before Cyrus was even born. Isaiah called Cyrus by name and confirmed that he was anointed by the Lord. If Iran's current supreme leader, Ayatollah Khamenei, was a good leader like Cyrus, then Jeremiah 49:34-39 would not be a NOW prophecy. The Lord would be pleased with the Ayatollah, rather than furious with him.

But why is the Lord fiercely angry with the government of Iran at the time of the prophecy? The reason is because Iran wants to launch something powerful somewhere. This is why the Lord will break the bow at the foremost of Iran's might in order to prevent such a lethal launch.

But where does Iran want to launch something powerful? Apparently, it wasn't Iraq because the Lord didn't prevent scores of Iranian missiles from landing in Iraq during the Iran-Iraq war of 1980-1988. Thus, it must be somewhere else, perhaps Israel. The prophecy doesn't tell us specifically where, but it does tell us that Iran has enemies, plural, when the prophecy happens.

This qualifies Israel today, because Iran has declared on numerous occasions that it wants to wipe Israel off of the map. Thus, it is safe to say that Israel and Iran are presently enemies. Should Iran get nuclear weapons, the destruction of Israel becomes a strong possibility. Even the attempted destruction of Israel is not something the Lord will tolerate!

Ezekiel 39:7 declares that the Lord is going to uphold His holy name through His people Israel, but if Iran nukes and destroys Israel prior to this war, the Lord's plan to uphold His holy name through Israel would be impossible! Ezekiel 39:7 would be unfulfillable and the Lord, rather than Iran, would be humiliated. Now do you see why the Lord is presently angry with the Iranian leadership? They must be stopped from destroying Israel, and they will be stopped!

The GCC (Gulf Cooperation Council of Arab states), which includes Saudi Arabia, Kuwait, Bahrain, Qatar, United Arab Emirates (UAE) and Oman, are deeply concerned about Iran's rogue regime, unchecked nuclear program and attempts to spread its hegemony throughout the entire Middle East. These GCC countries, in addition to Israel, presently constitute part of the plurality of Iran's enemies as predicted in Jeremiah 49:37.

The Iranians and their proxies are primarily Shiite Muslims, but the GCC states are predominately Sunnis. For centuries there have been infightings between these two Islamic factions. A nuclear weaponized Iran could easily advance Iran's stronghold in the Middle East. Iran already controls most of Lebanon through Hezbollah, Yemen with the Houthis, Syria via Bashar al-Assad and his

Alawite regime and much of Southern Iraq through the present Iraqi government.

Of greater or equal concerns to the GCC Arab states is the fact that they are heavily dependent upon the Persian Gulf for their drinkable and potable water needs. An estimated two-thirds of the world's desalinization plants exist in these GCC countries. They are oil rich, but water poor. They need the waters from the gulf in order to survive.

They are so concerned about the potential for a nuclear disaster emanating from the Bushehr nuclear reactor that they conducted an expansive study on the threats it poses to their nations. They released their findings in July, 2013. Below is a July 24, 2013, quote from Al Arabiya about the GCC findings.

"Iranian radiation a threat to GCC water security?"

"The risk of radiation from Iran's Bushehr nuclear power plant, if there is an accident, is extremely high to the GCC states. Studies and analyses suggest that any leak from the plant will affect the GCC's water supplies especially desalinization plant operation. In the event of a radiation leak, clouds of radioactive material will drift to the GCC states in just 15 hours. While the radiation would affect only about 10 percent of the Iranian population, in the GCC states, 40 to 100 percent of the population would be affected."[4]

This committee assessed that the greatest potential threat from Bushehr to the Arab Gulf States was to their water supply. The quote above posits the dangerous possibility that in less than a day's time, that 100% of their populations could be adversely affected by a nuclear disaster from Bushehr.

Below is another quote from an article dated July 31, 2013, that was written about the water concerns of the GCC. This report provides information about their future plans to protect themselves from a nuclear disaster across the gulf in Iran.

"In mid-July, the GCC Secretariat General announced plans for the construction of a joint water supply system, which will reduce the overwhelming reliance of member states on the Arabian (Persian) Gulf as their primary water source. Few details have yet been released, but the GCC Assistant Economic Secretary, Abdullah al-Shibli, has said that 'the water link is to build a line from the Gulf of Oman to Kuwait, passing through the GCC countries.' The pipeline will utilize water from outside the Arabian Gulf and will include storage facilities to stock potable water and distribute drinkable supplies across member states. The logistics of the plan are not yet available and it is unclear whether the water will be desalinated in Oman then pumped to its GCC neighbors, or whether salt water will be pumped for utilization in domestic desalination plants…Planning and construction of the pipeline are now in the works and it is expected that the project could be ready by 2020, at a cost of US$7 billion."[5]

Some cost estimates to complete this project are as high as 10.5 billion.[6] Knowing all these GCC concerns, I think it's safe to say that the GCC states are also currently enemies of Iran.

The Lord is Fiercely Angry with Iran

The Lord is angry with Iran for at least two primary reasons. The first was previously discussed concerning Iran's stated intentions to wipe Israel off of the map. However, the second is the Iranian governments stepped up persecution of their Christian countrymen.

A few years ago, former Iranian president Mahmoud Ahmadinejad and Ayatollah Khamenei issued a decree to close all home churches, imprison all pastors and persecute all Christians. This ruthless behavior has increased with the advent of the JCPOA nuclear deal negotiated on July 14, 2015.

Converting to Christianity in Iran today is a guaranteed path to severe persecution, if not martyrdom, and yet Iran has the fastest growing evangelical population in the world. Miracles, dreams, visions, healings and other supernatural events are occurring frequently within Iran. This, coupled with Christian satellite television, is causing tens of thousands of Iranians to abandon Islam and embrace Christianity.

The one true God of the Bible, Who is about to uphold His holy name through His people Israel, is winning the hearts and souls of many Iranians. The Lord is single-handedly accomplishing His goal expressed in John 3:16 that He wants none to perish, but that all would have eternal life through faith in Christ. The Lord is personally going into repressed Islamic areas like Iran and Syrian refugee camps, places where missionaries can scarcely go, and getting the job of winning souls into His kingdom done.

But, the Supreme Leader of Iran, Ayatollah Khamenei, and his radical regime are proactively attempting to extinguish the growing flame of Christianity inside Iran. This cannot please the Lord!

The spiritual showdown occurring in Iran is a supernatural phenomenon that deserves a closer look. American Christians can grow their faith and gain great inspiration by learning more about what the Lord is doing in places like Iran, the Syrian refugee camps, China and elsewhere. The chapter entitled, "Spiritual Showdowns Are Happening NOW," explores some powerful stories and testimonies from people in these repressed areas that have been blessed supernaturally by the Lord.

In addition to the research provided in my *Nuclear Showdown in Iran book*, several related articles, and media programs can be accessed at my website, which is www.prophecydepot.com.

5

Spiritual Showdowns Are Happening NOW!

The inescapable theme throughout this book is the pronouncement that the God of the Bible is about to uphold His holy name through the His people Israel in fulfillment of Ezekiel 39:7. The world is about to receive this powerful wakeup call and be given the golden opportunity to offer their unadulterated adoration to the covenant keeping God of Abraham, Isaac, and Jacob. The promise keeping God whose great love caused Him to send His only begotten son Jesus Christ as an offering for mankind's sins.

The stage is presently being set for this main event. Prophecies are readying for their fulfillment, and spiritual showdowns throughout the globe are taking place NOW in preparation! The God of the Bible is currently challenging all of His god competitors to prove their worthiness of worship. The Lord is flushing them out and forcing them to disprove His multiple biblically declared claims, like in Isaiah 46:9-10, to be the one and only true God!

Miracles, healings, dreams, visions, personal encounters and biblical prophecies are a few of the supernatural methods being employed to authenticate His superiority. Moreover, the Lord is not doing all the above to show off, rather to show up and share His love for the lost. The Lord is not constrained to prove Himself before the god imposters; rather He is compelled to prevent people from perishing in these last days. It is His love that always drives His actions!

"He who does not love does not know God, for God is love."

— 1 John 4:8

"For God so loved the world that He gave His only begotten Son, (Jesus Christ) that whoever believes in Him
should not perish but have everlasting life."

— John 3:16

Spiritual Showdowns Were Predicted to Happen

Zephaniah the prophet foretold of the coming of these spiritual showdowns.

"LORD *will be* awesome to them, For He will
reduce to nothing all the gods of the earth; *People*
shall worship Him, Each one from his place, Indeed
all the shores of the nations."

— Zephaniah 2:11

This verse, written about 625 B.C., introduces two prophecies. First, it declares that someday, the God, (capital G), of the Bible will eliminate all the false gods, (small g), presently worshipped
within the world. Second, this one true God will rightfully receive
His due praise throughout the entire earth. This global adoration
takes place when Christ returns and rules over the earth in His millennial reign, which means that the removal of the false gods must
take place sometime prior.

The Hebrew word used for "reduce to nothing" can be translated as, *famished, starved, emaciated* or *made lean*.[7] There are two
primary ways through which the Lord can accomplish this spectacular feat. One method is that He can *overrun* the pagan deities
and the other is that He can *overshadow* them. He appears to be
utilizing both techniques.

To *overrun* is to decisively defeat and occupy the territory of an enemy. In this process the competing god is overpowered, overthrown and proven unfit for further worship.

To *overshadow* is to tower tall above an object, which results in the casting of a shadow over it. In this example, it is the ability of the greater God to prove His prominence and superiority over the stature of the lesser god. To *overshadow* does not require the overrunning of an idol, rather it is accomplished by making the false god fail in a final choice comparison. It causes the devotee to question the object of his or her devotion. It deflects adulation away from the lying idol by alluring admiration to the obvious greater God.

As the Lord steps up His current campaign to overpower and overshadow all the false gods, followers of Hinduism, Buddhism and other mostly passive religions will have to deal with major theological differences between Christianity and their respective religions. One by one, the pagan deities will succumb to the supremacy of the Lord, and when He upholds His holy name through the nation of Israel in Ezekiel 39:7, everyone dwelling upon the earth at that time will be forced to focus on His sovereign power!

With this in mind, the Zephaniah 2:11 prophecies could be paraphrased to read as follows;

> *"The Lord will be awesome to them, For He will famish the false gods, which will evidence that they were all incompetent and unworthy of any worship. Instead, people will praise the one true God that overpowers and overshadows all the others."*

This chapter will demonstrate that the spiritual showdowns are currently underway. However, it is the fulfillment of Zephaniah 2:11 that officially commences the final elimination process of all the false gods. Thus, it is important to understand the context and timing of the fulfillment of Zephaniah 2:8-11. This prophecy appears to connect with the toppling of Jordan for its participation in the Psalm 83 prophecy. The primary god worshipped in Jordan that stands to be adversely affected is Allah. More information about Zephaniah's prophecy is provided in the appendix entitled; "The Xenocide of the gods of the Earth." This appendix is written in my book called, *"Isralestine, The Ancient Blueprints of the Future Middle East."*

Among the plethora of pagan deities, Scriptures point out that two of the most prominent ones will be overrun. They are Allah and Satan. Allah appears to be represented in Zephaniah 2:9-11. In these verses, Zephaniah is dealing with the famishing of the god of the Jordanians, (historically Moab and Ammon). Today, the primary god worshipped by most Jordanians is Allah.

Revelation 12:7-9 states that Michael the Archangel and his heavenly armies will win a war against Satan and his fallen angels. This defeat casts Satan and his cohorts down from heaven to the earth. This is followed a few years later by the prophecy in Revelation 20:1-2, which informs that an angel eventually overpowers Satan and binds him in chains for 1000 years in the bottomless pit. These predictions concerning Satan find fulfillment during the LAST prophecies period. They are neither NOW or NEXT events.

Allah is Losing His Akbar (His claim to the greatest god).

Allah, on the other hand, is already finding it difficult to maintain stability within his religion of Islam. The infighting in the Middle East between the Shia's and Sunnis is causing places like Syria, Iraq and Yemen to implode. As a result, many Muslims are beginning to question *Allah's Akbar.*

Future Muslim defeats in the wars of Psalm 83 and Ezekiel 38 will serve devastating blows to Allah. In Psalm 83:9-11, the IDF appears to be empowered militarily to defeat the surrounding Arab nations and terrorist groups. Subsequently, in Ezekiel 38:18-39:6, the LORD supernaturally defeats the outer ring of nations identified in Ezekiel 38:1-5. These appear to be two distinctly different prophetic events involving two separate predominately Muslim coalitions.

Ultimately, Allah will be *overrun,* but presently this pagan god is being *overshadowed.* The Lord is accomplishing amazing things in several Muslim countries causing many to willingly forfeit their faith in Islam. Allah's appeal is fading fast. Neither can he control the growing chaos within his religion, nor can he match up with the supernatural miracles, healings, visions and dreams being outsourced from the Lord. Christ is standing tall and casting His shadow over Allah who is steadily shrinking small!

Disillusioned Muslims are abandoning Allah and converting to Christianity in record numbers. This is taking place in Iran, Saudi Arabia, the Syrian refugee camps, and other repressed places throughout the Muslim world.

Iran is a perfect example of this. Christianity is burgeoning in Iran and as a result the government is aggressively clamping down on it. Nationwide, Bibles are being confiscated, home churches are being shut down and Christians are being thrown in jail for their faith. The Iranian government is even targeting those with dual citizenship to make sure they are not promoting political dissidence or spreading Christianity.

In many cases the Christians are being beaten to a pulp and given no medical treatment or legal representation. The intentions of the thrashings are that the Christians will die from organ failures or other related causes. I know about this mistreatment from personal sources involved in the underground church of Iran. Over the past couple of years the repression has increased dramatically. This Christian persecution intensified during the nuclear negotiation process between Iran and the P5+1, (Russia, China, USA, UK, France plus Germany). The deal was negotiated on July 14, 2015, but the beatings still continue to be severe.

Why are these Iranians and so many other Muslims worldwide renouncing Islam and converting to Christianity? The fact is, Islam is not working for many Muslims, but Jesus Christ is! I mean, He really is, literally not figuratively! As you are about to find out, Christ is personally proactively interacting with many of these disillusioned Muslims.

Christ is frequently visiting the repressed areas of the world. He is blatantly disregarding the decrees of despotic governments and is entering into dangerous countries where missionaries can scarcely go. People are experiencing supernatural encounters on an intimate level with the Lord. The Lord is making His move now, which implies that time is short and the harvest field is ripe.

As a religion, Islam is guilty of overpromising, but under delivering. Many Muslims are losing hope and looking outside of Islam for religious truth and the way to live a truly fulfilling life. Jesus realizes this and since He is the way, the truth and the life according to John 14:6, He is seizing the opportunity to reach out to them in their times of despair.

Christ knows that He is the good news that they are looking for, but His emissaries, i.e. Christian missionaries, are being severely restricted by tyrannical governments from traveling into the places where they are desperately needed. Do any of you want to walk into the headquarters of the ISIS terrorist group as a Christian evangelist?

Jesus realizes this is not a tour of duty at the top of a missionaries list, yet somehow the good news about God's love for the oppressed has to be communicated to them. So, Christ is using every means available to Him to transmit the message of His love to the lost. Supernatural acts, like miracles, dreams, visions and healings are being utilized alongside the technological resources of satellite television and the Internet to reach the oppressed. It is spiritual warfare at an unprecedented level.

Iran Has Become a Spiritual Battleground

A spiritual showdown between Christianity and Islam has been ongoing since the ruthless regime of former Ayatollah Khomeini came into power during the Iranian revolution in 1979. At that time, there were an estimated 500 Christians living in Iran. It is difficult to know how many Christians there are now, but some estimates are as high as 5 million. If this is an accurate number, it represents a ten-thousand fold increase in fewer than forty years.

Many Iranians supported the Islamic takeover on the hopes that a nation governed by Sharia law would provide them a better future. Immediately upon coming into power, the Ayatollah and his mullahs attempted to spread their hegemony into Iraq. This led to a war of attrition with Iraq from 1980-1988. Those eight years took a heavy toll on Iran religiously, economically, militarily and politically. It forced the radical regime to tighten its grip over the people to maintain all aspects of its power.

Today the vast majority of Iranians were born after the 1979 revolution and they have become victimized by this dictatorial leadership. Many of these Iranians have become disillusioned with their Islamic leaders and their breed of radical Islam.

Through the Internet, satellite television and various other means, this younger generation has been able to look outside the restrictions of state censored media and seventh century Islam into what's going on in other parts of the world. In many instances they like what they see. However, much of what they like is strictly forbidden in Iran. For instance, a woman walking in public without her hijab (headdress) can land her in jail. Also, promoting westernized music and dance can get you 91 lashes and possible jail time.[8]

The Lord is reaching into the homes and hearts of millions of Iranians through the supernatural and technological means already mentioned. His methods are having an inescapable impact. The government is having limited success in preventing the spread of Christianity through the technologies, but no success in stopping the supernatural events. Below are a few examples that demonstrate what the Lord is doing to communicate His love to the downtrodden in Iran.

Bibles Are Blessing Iranians

The Ayatollah won't tolerate the circulation of Bibles inside Iran, but Christ is personally making sure that His Holy Word is being translated into Farsi and delivered into many Iranian hands. Maryam Rostampour and Marziyeh Amirizadeh, affectionately referred to by many Iranian Christians as M & M, are a classic example of this. In 2009, they were arrested for distributing 20,000 Bibles, mostly inside of Tehran. Their gripping story is detailed in their thrilling book entitled, *Captive in Iran.*

Captive in Iran provides an inside look at the severity of the Christian persecution in Iran. I have read it and highly recommend it.[9] M & M were sentenced to death and sent to the Evin prison. This prison, Iran's worst, is a place where inmates are routinely tortured, and executions are swift and sudden. During their stay at Evin, M & M began preaching the gospel, singing praises to God and praying for many of the female inmates. Essentially, they were converting Iran's worst prison into a church at some levels. Their testimony is very reminiscent of the Apostles accounts written in the book of Acts chapters 5, 12 and 16.

This behavior aggravated the prison authorities who continued to treat M & M harshly. However, that didn't stop them from ministering inside the prison walls. Ultimately, after 259 days they were released because public outcry for them had grown to an embarrassingly high level for the Iranian authorities.

But why would M & M and Iranian Christians like them attempt to pass out Bibles and spread Christianity inside Iran knowing that they could be imprisoned, tortured, raped and even killed? I asked this question of my friend Hormoz Shariat, the founder of Iran Alive

Ministries.[10] Hormoz, who author Joel Rosenberg calls the "Billy Graham of Iran," is the founder of a 24/7 satellite channel broadcast that transmits into the Middle East. I have been on his show several times teaching about some of the prophecies in this book, which he translates into Farsi. Hormoz answered my question as follows,

> "Many Iranian Christian converts like M & M previously considered themselves dead in Islam. Islam offered them nothing, no hope and no future. This is why Iran has one of the highest suicide rates in the world. But, receiving Christ gave them renewed life, love, hope, peace, happiness and a future. Since they experience new life in Christ and previously reckoned themselves dead in Islam, they feel compelled to share the love of Christ with their fellow countrymen. They want to live for Christ even if it costs them their lives in the process."

Foreign missionaries may not be allowed into Iran, but the locals also find it difficult to get out of Iran. Many Iranians travel across the border into Turkey after converting to Christianity. Turkey allows Iranians to visit without a visa for up to three months. Home churches still exist in Turkey and they are a prime source for Christian discipleship. At the end of the three months, most Iranians come back to Iran. Many of them return with a burning zeal to preach the gospel and pass out Bibles.

What better missionaries could Christ send into the spiritual battlefield of Iran than these returnees? They know the language, culture and traditions of Iran, and they know the dangers of living under the ruthless Islamic regime in Iran.

Some of us believe that the exiles mentioned in Jeremiah 49:36 may be believers that preach the gospel into many of the world nations. The verse says that there will be no nations where these evacuees will not go. These refugees will be able to boldly proclaim throughout the world that they are the witnesses of a fulfilled ancient prophecy in Jeremiah 49:34-39. If this prophecy finds fulfillment before the Rapture, then this could definitely be the case. If the Rapture happens prior to Jeremiah's prophecy, then these believers will already be caught up into heaven. However, their mantle could be, and probably will be, picked up by Iranian unbelievers that are left behind, but become believers afterwards.

The Mystery Man and His Iranian Scribe

This story of M & M is one of the several ways the Lord is circulating His word inside of Iran, but below is a miraculous story about another method the Lord is utilizing to this end. This is a personal testimony from Mansour. Mansour is a disciple of Hormoz Shariat and is one of the leaders of the underground church inside Iran. Mansour, which is not his real name, is connected with about 4000 Iranian Christians. His anonymity is protected because of his high pastoral profile inside Iran. Below is a recent email of a personal testimony that he shared with me.

"Hi Bill, Here is an amazing story.

I was in a city that is very famous for heroin. Heroin is so rampant that it's cheaper than bread. I was in this city and a believer said you have to meet this man and hear about his mysterious story. We took a taxi and traveled outside of the city. We went into the country on the road that drug dealers frequently use to smuggle drugs.

It was mostly a dirt road and we drove for about an hour. We arrived at a house that had no electricity, no gas, no telephone and no satellite TV. We walked in and observed that it was basically just a mud house, which is not uncommon in some of the impoverished rural areas of Iran. We sat down on a dirt filled floor and the man residing there told us the following story."

"A mysterious man wearing all white with a long beard came to my house late one night. He knocked and when I opened the door his appearance was so overwhelming that I couldn't look directly into His face. For the storyteller it was very weird that he was unable to look at His face, but he felt a peace about this man. (*Remember this is a drug smuggling road that is very dangerous*).

When he let the mysterious man in he said to him write this down. By candlelight the storyteller began to pen the words given to him from the mystery man. The writing stopped when the storyteller fell asleep. The same process commenced again several more times until the writing was completed."

"I asked him what did He ask you to write down and he brought his notebook. It was the whole book of John verbatim, PERFECT. Then the man said to me that the stranger had said, "*I am the Way and the Life.*" "The story-teller asked me who is this man who claims to be the Way and the Life?"

"I read the man John 14:6, which says, "*I (Jesus Christ) am the way, the truth, and the life. No one comes to the Father except through Me.*" Then I proceeded to explain to him, and through his own notebook, that God visited him, that Jesus had personally visited him. He came to Christ and now is telling many people about Jesus."

This story and many more can be found on Mansour's website at: http://www.catalyticministries.com

For another powerful supernatural experience in Iran, I strongly recommend that you watch the YouTube video called, "Padina's Story." Padina, which is not her real name, is Mansour's wife. Her true story is one example of many that evidences what Jesus Christ is accomplishing inside Iran. Here is the link: https://www.youtube.com/watch?v=rVCj26fdJpQ

6

The Decline Of America

Decline of America

Creation of Israel		EZEKIEL 38
	68 YEARS	Ezekiel 38:13
1948	2016	20??

I t was Saturday night on December 5, 2015, and I was having dinner with Pastor Dave Barton, my son's father-in-law. Dining with us was 12 year old Brent, the son of a family friend.

Pastor Barton and I were planning on going to a movie theater after eating. But during the meal, 12 year old Brent asked me a seemingly innocent question," *Where do you like to sit in a movie theater?*" I replied, "*Towards the back so the screen isn't so big in front of me.*"

Brent responded, "*My father and I always sit in the back also!*" His tone was quite serious prompting me to ask, "*Why is that?*" Brent's response immediately removed all the innocence from his initial question. "*My father and I always sit in the back of the movie theater so we won't get shot from behind.*" Looking into the eyes of Pastor Dave, I said,

> "*Only in this generation! Only in this generation would you hear such a distressing comment coming out of the mouth of a 12 year old American boy. This was not a concern that any of us had at his age! We grew up during the "Ozzie and Har-*

riet," "My Three Sons," and "Father Knows Best" days of the 50's and 60's. We never worried about getting shot in public places. Those days most people didn't even lock their doors. But today, there's no sacred public place anymore in America. Mass serial killings take place in malls, theaters, marathons, churches, libraries, conference centers and more."

I shared this personal story for a couple of reasons. *First*, it identifies some of the growing concerns facing this generation. Similar types of conversations are commonly taking place at dinner tables throughout this country. Guns and ammunition sales, purchased for self-defense purposes, are at record levels as a result of these heightened concerns.

Second, it hopefully prompts the reader to recognize that times are worsening, rather than improving. I often ask people that are concerned about what's taking place in America and throughout the world, "Do you think things will get better?" The answer is usually an emphatic "NO," or in some instances, "things will get worse before they get better." Let me ask you the same question. What do you think? Will things continue to deteriorate here and abroad? If we are living in the biblical last days, the answer must be a resounding YES!

Lastly, I want the reader to flash back in time and imagine the dining room experiences of a few important historical figures. Pull up a chair at Noah's dinner table, when he informed his family that world conditions were so bad that the Lord was going to flood the earth. Seat yourself at the banquet of Belshazzar, the Babylonian king, when Daniel told him that the mysterious writing on the wall predicted the immediate collapse of his kingdom. According to Daniel 5:30-31, the king was slain and Babylon was conquered that very night.

If you believe that the prophecies explored thus far are rightfully classified as NOW prophecies, then your frame of mind should be similar to the following Old Testament examples;

- Abraham, when he heard that Sodom and Gomorrah was going to be destroyed, which is where his nephew Lot and his family resided. (Genesis 18:16-33),

- The Pharaoh of Egypt, when Joseph warned that after seven years of plenty, seven years of famine would follow and utterly deplete the land. (Genesis 41:25-30),

- The king of Nineveh, when Jonah the prophet warned him that his kingdom was about to perish within forty days. (Jonah 3:4),

- The people of Judea, when Jeremiah warned them that they were about to go into seventy years of Babylonian captivity. (Jeremiah 25:11).

Envision what it would be like to have been the *fly on the wall* during these powerful discussions. These stern forewarnings warranted serious mindsets among those destined to be adversely affected. For the individuals who took these admonitions to heart, their outlooks rapidly changed drastically.

Noah and his family began building an ark. Abraham pleaded for mercy on Sodom and Gomorrah if at least ten righteous people dwelt there. Joseph and many of his countrymen embarked upon a seven year food storage campaign. The king of Nineveh made a public proclamation calling for a national repentance throughout the Assyrian empire. Many Judeans accepted their foretold fate and began preparing for their prolonged period of captivity.

The people in these examples above appreciated, and acted upon, the prophetic word of God. The invaluable information they received prompted them to prepare for what was forthcoming. Likewise, if you appreciate the prophetic word of God, then you should also have your important dinner table discussions and begin planning ahead for what the Bible forewarns is coming. There are necessary preparations that you can take now to get ready for what is about to happen!

What about America's Future?

For Americans, the next three chapters are the most important ones within this book. They address the core national spiritual and moral matters that are near and dear to American hearts. These powerful chapters explore the geopolitical, biblical and prophetic reasons that suggest America will decline from its superpower status as a NOW prophecy. These chapters should prompt you to prepare NOW for America's decline. Don't procrastinate, the adage to adopt is; *"Don't put off until tomorrow, what you can do today!"*

Scoffers and Skeptics

Due to the sensitive subject matter contained in these three chapters, some readers might receive this information with skepticism, or flatly scoff at the teachings entirely. Many Americans are in denial about the present depraved condition of their country. Even though several important Supreme Court decisions since the 1960's have transgressed over numerous dangerous biblical boundaries, they still think God parades about in heaven singing the Star Spangled Banner while being draped in the American flag.

This type of resistant mentality is to be expected, hopefully not because the teachings of this chapter are erroneous, ambiguous or unclear, but because the skeptical and scoffing mindsets are not open to receive the Bible based research provided. The historical heroes and heroines above often met with similar attitudes as they sounded their prophetic alarms and made their appropriate preparations.

Naysayers would commonly scoff and ridicule their behaviors. These scorners were usually destroyed when the crisis came. 2 Peter 3:3 warns that this attitude will also exist in the end times. This group will mostly be characterized with a *"Wait and see"* attitude. Unfortunately, they may *wait* only to *see* that it's far too late to prepare, as it was for Lot's relatives who thought he was joking when warning them about impending judgment (Genesis 19:14).

Apathy is another potential attitude to address. Skeptics and even those who embrace the teachings in these three chapters still must decide when and how to respond to America's decline. The adages that this group should adopt are; *"Act now, because it's better to be safe than sorry,"* and *"It's now or never."* I encourage those of you with this outlook to *act now;* because you may soon become *sorry* that you will *never be safe* again.

Is America in the Bible?

It was about 8:00 a.m. on Saturday morning on August 8, 2015, when I shared with my good friend Dr. David Reagan, the prophetic basis for supporting America's imminent decline from superpower status. Dr. Reagan, the founder of Lamb and Lion Ministries and the host of the Christ in Prophecy TV show, and I were having breakfast together at the time.[11] We were both scheduled to deliver timely messages at the Al Gist's, Maranatha Evangelical Ministries, prophecy conference later that day.[12]

Before I recap our breakfast discussion, let me provide you with a couple of quotes from Dr. David Reagan about his perspective concerning America's current spiritual condition. These Reagan quotes were published before our breakfast conversation.

> *"I believe the trigger point for our nation occurred in November 2012 when President Obama was re-elected. We have ignored the prophets and the remedial judgments. God has responded by giving us the kind of leader we deserve. We are now positioned to be delivered from Judgment to Destruction."*[13]

> *"Note the date: June 26, 2015. (The day that the Supreme Court upheld same sex marriages) It is the date that should*

*be put on the headstone of our nation because it is the day
that America died. We have sealed our destruction. We are
now a walking-dead nation."[14]*

The Reagan / Salus Conversation

Bill: "David, you believe that America is presently operating
under God's judgment, and possibly even positioned to be
delivered from judgment to destruction, is that correct?"

David: "Yes I do."

Bill: "I am in total agreement with you about this! Am I correct to presume that your primary reasons for this view-
point are primarily based upon the premises that America
has transgressed all the biblical boundaries, which other
nations and empires that crossed them were judged for?
Also, because America has ignored the remedial judgments and prophetic voices that God has sent as warnings
to this nation?"

David: "Yes again."

Bill: "So, your conclusions are mostly based upon biblical
and historical precedent along with current geo-political
events, is that correct?"

David: "Yes, mostly."

Bill: "What about the prophetic perspective? Do you believe
America is identified in Bible prophecy in a compromised
capacity, like in a less than a superpower status condition?"

David: "No, I am not convinced that America is identified in the
Bible prophetically."

Bill: "I believe America is identified in a lesser capacity prophetically in Ezekiel 38:13, as the 'Young lions of the merchants of Tarshish.' These young lions appear to be merely
protesting the Gog of Magog invasion of Israel politically,
rather than preventing it militarily. This leads me to believe that America is portrayed in this prophecy as a weak-
er nation than we are presently. I believe that I can provide
sufficient biblical, geopolitical and prophetic information
that argues a good case for America being identified in a
lesser condition within the Bible."

David: "I would be curious to find out more about your research
into this topic."

Bill: "The reason that the prophetic perspective is important; is
because it mutes the arguments that can be levied against
our conclusions about America's present judgment predicament."

David: "What arguments?"

Bill: "Some could contend that America is still a Christian
nation that continues to be blessed with superpower status. The country is filled with many good church-going
Christians that are serving the Lord. They could carry
the argument further by asking, "Why would God judge
this God-fearing nation that is still doing His bidding?
Wouldn't that be like shooting Himself in the foot?""

"They might also reason, "Certainly, non-Christian nations like China, with its human rights issues, or some
Islamic countries like Syria, where ISIS is beheading
Christians, deserve God's judgment, but America's not
that bad in comparison. The historical examples of fallen
empires show that they deserved their fates; they were bad
throughout their entire societies, which is not presently
the case throughout America.""

"In the cases above it mostly comes down to the Abrahamic rationale in Genesis 18:23 when he questioned God concerning the impending judgment of Sodom and Gomorrah, *"Would You also destroy the righteous with the wicked?"* In Genesis 18:32 Abraham had persuaded God to relent from judging the cities if only ten righteous people resided there. *"Then he said, "Let not the Lord be angry, and I will speak but once more: Suppose ten (righteous) should be found there?" And He (the Lord) said, "I will not destroy it for the sake of ten."* We know that the ten did not exist, but there are hundreds of thousands, if not millions of true Christians dwelling in America.""

"Then there is the pro-Israel argument, which points out that America is still Israel's greatest ally. Genesis 12:3 promises to bless those that bless Abraham, which carries on down to his Hebrew descendants, the Jewish people of today."

David: "Are you going to be presenting your prophetic proofs about America in your presentation today?"

Bill: "I wasn't initially, but I will as a result of our discussion. If it can be proven that we live in the last days, and that in these last days America is identified in a lesser capacity prophetically, then Americans will have to take our conclusions to heart. They can raise the arguments above, but then they have to answer the question as to why America appears to be a lesser nation in the end times according to the Bible?"

The presentation from that day did include the prophetic reasons that I believe supports the decline of America in the end times. In fact, that presentation is incorporated into the *NOW Prophecies* DVD that correlates with this book.

Identifying a lesser America in Bible prophecy

This section explores one of the two potential prophetic reasons that America becomes a lesser nation in the end times. One is an indirect inference from which a conclusion can be drawn through the process of deductive reasoning, and the other is a direct reference that I believe can be scripturally supported. The direct reference is explained in the chapter entitled, "Is America in Ezekiel 38?"

The indirect reference is biblically supported, but requires an understanding of the prophetic role of the revived Roman Empire in the end times. In this scenario America is locatable, but not directly identifiable.

The Bible predicts that the Roman Empire would reemerge in the end times. It is commonly taught by respected Bible prophecy teachers, like Hal Lindsey, Dr. David Reagan, Dr. Dr. Arnold Fruchtenbaum and a host of others, that the four primary Gentile empires identified in the book of Daniel represent Babylon, Medo-Persia, Greece and Rome. History supports this teaching.

The descriptions of the Roman Empire in Daniel 7:7-8 and elsewhere in Scripture lead me and these teachers to conclude that the Roman Empire, although it fell, would be revived in the end times. The European Union appears to have come into existence on route to the fulfillment of this revived empire. The deductive reasoning is as follows;

> *Major Premise:* If the ancient Roman Empire reemerges to play a significant, perhaps superpower, role in the end times, then other superpower competitors will likely decline in their prominence. As the Roman Empire revives, America as a superpower should decline.

> *Minor Premise:* America is not necessarily part of the revived Roman Empire, which encourages the possibility

that its superpower status will someday slip away. The fact that America consists of a vast conglomeration of immigrants, many from European descent, does not necessarily qualify it as part of the former Roman Empire, which was based out of Rome.

This indirect scenario has merit and some biblical support, but does not conclusively evidence that America's superpower status will diminish in the end times. Therefore, it is important to specifically identify America prophetically in the Bible to see if such a conclusion can decisively be drawn.

How Romans 1:18-32 Applies to AMERICA NOW!

The chapter called, "Will Americans Perish from Lack of Prophetic Knowledge?" provides the biblical basis and historical precedent for the decline of America. That chapter evidences how, over the past five decades, Americans have essentially removed God from almost every important aspect of their culture and society. As such, it has been argued by some of today's top Bible teachers, including myself, that the country now falls into the Romans 1:18-32 categories.

These telling verses explain what happens to individuals, but more importantly, to nations that transgress the bottom-line biblical boundaries established by God. In his book entitled, *The Late Great United States*, Dr. Mark Hitchcock explains these verses as follows:

> *"Romans 1:18-25 sets forth the character and cause of God's judgment against a civilization. In short, these verses tell us that when people willfully reject God, He eventually reveals His wrath against them. People can't turn their backs on God with impunity."*[15]

The divine judgment against the transgressing nation unfolds in three digressive stages. First, the people are *given over* to sexual perversion, the *"lusts of their hearts."* (Romans 1:24). In America, this stage seemingly began in the 1960's when the sexual revolution began, which interestingly enough, occurred after the Supreme Court banned Bible reading and prayer from our schools. In 1973, when the Supreme Court legalized abortion, the accountability of responsible sexual behavior became minimized, by eliminating the burdens of child birthing and child rearing. Correspondingly, in the 1970's, more permissive legislation permitted the rise of adult theaters in the United States.[16] This period was known as "The Golden Age of Porn."[17]

Second, the population is *given over* to homosexuality, "*vile passions.*" (Romans 1:26). This has been developing since the 1970's, but became blatantly observable in the past two decades. In 2003, the *Lawrence v. Texas* case was a landmark decision by the United States Supreme Court, which struck down the sodomy law in Texas and, by extension, invalidated sodomy laws in 13 other states, making same-sex sexual activity legal in every U.S. state and territory.

In 2013, the Supreme Court struck down a key part of the 1996 Defense of Marriage Act (DOMA). DOMA defended the constitutionality of marriage as being between one man and one woman. DOMA is the biblically supported view according to Genesis 2:24 and Matthew 19:5-6. This Supreme Court decision paved the way for their approval of same sex marriages on June 26, 2015. This is the Supreme Court decision that prompted Dr. Reagan to state, "*We have sealed our destruction. We are now a walking-dead nation.*"

Finally, individuals as well as societies are *given over* to moral decadence, "*a debased mind.*" (Romans 1:28). This process is what Isaiah 5:20 warns against when it says; "Woe to those who call evil good, and good evil; Who put darkness for light, and light for darkness; Who put bitter for sweet, and sweet for bitter!"

This third and final stage of unrighteousness will characterize America's future unless a major spiritual change occurs in the hearts and minds of Americans. The Bible explains the condition much better than I can.

"And even as they did not like to retain God in *their* knowledge, God gave them over to a debased mind, to do those things which are not fitting; being filled with all unrighteousness, sexual immorality, wickedness, covetousness, maliciousness; full of envy, murder, strife, deceit, evil-mindedness; *they are* whisperers, backbiters, haters of God, violent, proud, boasters, inventors of evil things, disobedient to parents, undiscerning, untrustworthy, unloving, unforgiving, unmerciful; who, knowing the righteous judgment of God, that those who practice such things are deserving of death, not only do the same but also approve of those who practice them." (Romans 1:28-32)

Some believe that America is already neck deep in the mire of debauchery, and as such, the nation has crossed the point of no return. There are a few questions that can be asked in this regard. If the honest answers are yes, then it implies that America is already spiritually and morally destitute.

- Is America still a Christian nation? (According to President Obama, "*we are no longer just a Christian nation*").[18]
- Have we kicked God out of our public schools, by removing prayer and Bible reading?
- Have we legalized abortion?
- Have we approved same sex marriages?
- Has greed, rather than God, become our main motivator?
- Have we turned our back on Israel? (Israeli Prime Minister Netanyahu diabolically opposes the nuclear deal with Iran that is supported by President Obama).

These are just a few core questions that hit at the heart of the national matter. Subjectively speaking, some readers may answer NO to a few of these questions. Objectively speaking, we should ponder how God would respond to these inquiries. When we use Romans 1:18-32 as a litmus test to what's taking place in America, the apparent answer from the Lord's perspective is, YES TO ALL THE ABOVE!

7

Will Americans Perish From Lack Of Prophetic Knowledge?

"My people perish from lack of knowledge."
— Hosea 4:6

I t was Thursday, September 17, 2015, at about 5:00 p.m., when I expressed my concerns to Dr. Chuck Missler that America was entering into a Hosea 4:6 moment. Dr. Missler is the founder of Koinonia House Ministries and one of today's top Bible prophecy experts. In fact, it was Dr. Missler that led me to Christ in 1990, while I was attending his classes on the book of Revelation at the Calvary Chapel in Big Bear Lake, CA.

Dr. Missler and I were having dinner together in the green room of the Jim Bakker TV studios when I shared my thoughts about America. We were there taping television shows for the Jim Bakker Prophetic Conference of 2015.

The timely table talk included some biblical references in 2 Chronicles 7:14, Jeremiah 7:16 and Hosea 4:6, which are explained in greater detail later in this chapter.

Bill: "Chuck, I have heard through the grapevine that you believe America is currently past the 2 Chronicles 7:14 stage, is that true?"

Chuck: "Yes, this is my concern.'"

Bill: "I wholeheartedly agree. If 2 Chronicles 7:14 is no longer applicable for the USA, this implies that America is past the point of having a Nineveh moment."

Chuck: "Yes, the Lord relented from destroying that city, because the people of Nineveh heeded the prophet Jonah's warnings and repented. In order for this process to be repeated in the USA, Americans would also need to repent, which probably won't happen."

Bill: "This means that America is presently experiencing a Jeremiah 7:16 moment."

Chuck: "What do you mean?"

Bill: "The southern kingdom of Judah became so wicked that the Lord told Jeremiah, *"Therefore, do not pray for this people, nor lift up a cry or prayer for them, nor make intercession to Me; for I will not hear you."* This meant that, in the Lord's foreknowledge, He knew that Judah would not have a Nineveh moment. Certainly, if the Judeans would have repented, the Lord would have continued to allow Jeremiah to make intercession for them. However, the Lord foreknew that no such repentance was forthcoming. From that point forward, Jeremiah was instructed to prophesy about the coming seventy years of Babylonian captivity."

Chuck: "Yes, that makes sense."

Bill: "Taking it to the next level then, if Jeremiah 7:16 now applies for America, Americans need to prepare NOW for having a Hosea 4:6 moment."

Chuck: "What do you mean?"

Bill: "If the USA, like Judah, is not going to repent and repeat the Nineveh experience, then Americans need to prepare for impending judgment. Hosea 4:6 warns that unprepared people will perish when judgment overtakes them. This appears to apply to everyone, whether they are believers or unbelievers."

Chuck: "That's an interesting assessment." Grabbing a pen and a table napkin, he asked, "What did you say that Scripture sequence was again?"

Dr. Missler wrote the verses down and took them to heart. The rest of this chapter is devoted to developing the possibility that America has past the point of no return, and like the historical examples above, needs to prepare for national judgment.

Throughout history, nations and empires have been judged and destroyed for transgressing biblically defined moral and spiritual boundaries! Boundaries such as:

- SEXUAL PERVERSION, like that of Sodom and Gomorrah at the time of Abraham around 2000 BC.

- IDOL WORSHIP, that in its worst conditions led to child sacrifice, which resulted in the destruction of the Northern Kingdom of Israel in 722 BC.

- WICKEDNESS AND MORAL DECADENCE, which caused the destruction of the Assyrian empire about 612 BC by the Babylonians and Medes.

- ANTI-SEMITISM, which led to the destruction of the Egyptian army at the time of Moses about 3500 BC.

In every instance the destructions caused unbearable sufferings and hardships to everyone, including believers in God and unbelievers that did not heed the prophetic warnings given in advance by the Hebrew prophets.

America is in the Danger Zone

Over the past fifty years, America has crossed all of these dangerous biblical boundaries:

- 1962 – Engel v. Vitale: the removal of Prayer in public schools by the Supreme Court.

- 1963 - Abington School District v. Schempp: the removal of Bible reading in public schools by the Supreme Court.

- 1973 - Rowe v. Wade: legalized abortions by the Supreme Court. Since then, America has performed over 55 million abortions. Presently about one million abortions are occurring per year in America.

- 1980 - Stone v. Graham: in this case the Supreme Court ruled that a Kentucky statute was unconstitutional. The statute in question required the posting of a copy of the Ten Commandments on the wall of each public classroom in the state. The Court ruled that because they were being placed in public classrooms they were in violation of the First Amendment.

- 2003 - Lawrence v. Texas: This was the landmark decision by the United States Supreme Court that struck down the sodomy law in Texas, which by extension, invalidated sodomy laws in 13 other states.

- 2013 - United States v. Windsor: the case that the Supreme Court struck down the Defense of Marriage Act (DOMA). DOMA stated that one man should be married to one woman. DOMA was biblically supported according to Genesis 2:24, "Therefore a man shall leave his father and mother and be joined to his wife, and they shall become one flesh."

- 2015 – Obergefell v. Hodges: the Supreme Court case that ruled in favor of Same Sex Marriages, which is unbiblical according to Romans 1:27 and elsewhere.

- 2015 – The present White House Administration has turned its back on Israel. As an example, Obama believes the Iran JCPOA nuclear deal is good, but Israeli Prime Minister Netanyahu believes it's the worst deal imaginable.

The Lord has provided ample warnings to Americans that the country is headed for destruction. These forewarning have come in the forms of remedial judgments, prophetic voices, and ultimately by giving them the ungodly leaders they deserve. For instance, U.S. President Barack Hussein Obama is the most pro-abortion, pro-homosexual, and anti-Israel president in America's history! His reelection for a second term evidences the spiritual and moral bankruptcy of the nation! These prophetic warnings are detailed in my DVD, "*America and the Coming Mideast Wars.*"

Presently, many people are heeding these God-given harbingers by either prepping in America for hard times, or departing from America for safer countries. In these titanic times, they don't want to sink with the American ship. Presently, I don't plan on leaving the country, but there are certain circumstances when that is a wise option. A few biblical examples are listed below.

In the past;

- Genesis 7:7-24 - Noah and his family boarded the ark to escape the flood that was coming upon the earth.

- Genesis 19:15-17 - Lot and his family evacuated out of Sodom, before the destruction of Sodom and Gomorrah.

In the present;

- Isaiah 17:1 – Damascus is predicted to be destroyed and non-existent in the future. This prophecy seems to be nearing its fulfillment. In my estimation it is presently advisable to depart from Damascus in advance of its desolation, which according to Isaiah 17:9, 14 happens overnight and is caused by the Israeli Defense Forces (I.D.F.).

- Jeremiah 49:34-39 – Iran (Elam) is going to experience a disaster that will force mass evacuation from the area. The details of the prophecy suggest that it is a nuclear disaster resulting in a humanitarian crisis. In light of the high probability that the I.D.F. is going to strike Iran's nuclear program soon, it would be wise to vacate from the territory now, before the calamity occurs.

In the future;

- Matthew 24:15-19 – Christ warns the Jews that in the middle of the 7-year Tribulation Period, to flee immediately from Jerusalem when they witness the Antichrist desecrating their third temple. This event triggers the final genocidal attempt of the Jews, which Zechariah 13:8 warns will lead to the killing of two-thirds of the Jewish population in the land of Israel. The advisable anticipatory move for all Jews living there at that time is to seek safety far in advance of this predicted event.

Stay Alive or Struggle to Survive

In the cases of the present and future prophetic scenarios, people can leave or prep now while they are alive, or struggle to exist in the harsh circumstances afterward should they survive. Unfortunately, not everyone has the financial wherewithal to leave now, so they could prepare a layered exit strategy. Perhaps they have friends or family living out of harm's way that they can make advanced preparations to go to in the event of an emergency. Also, everyone should maintain active passports in case they are confronted with a crisis that causes them to flee across international borders.

Should Americans still hope in 2 Chronicles 7:14?

Over the past several decades, many Christians have been sounding the 2 Chronicles 7:14 warning throughout America, which reads;

> "If My people who are called by My name will humble
> themselves, and pray and seek My face, and turn from
> their wicked ways, then I will hear from heaven, and will
> forgive their sin and heal their land."[19]

Although these verses dealt with the Lord's response to King Solomon's petition for the protection of the nation of Israel, the hope was that they could also find application in America. The reasoning was that if American Christians would humble themselves, pray, turn away from evil and seek the Lord that they could bring God's favor upon their nation.

Whether or not this presumption was correct, it does not appear to be working presently in the USA. The sobering reality is that, while the 2 Chronicles mantra was being echoed throughout the nation, the Lord was issuing remedial judgments that a majority of Americans and their leaders have continued to ignore.

Can America still have a Nineveh Moment?

Nineveh, the capital city of the Assyrian empire was ultimately destroyed around 612 BC; however the empire had become exceedingly evil long before it came to its end. At the height of its wickedness, the Lord sent the prophet Jonah to warn of its impending destruction. Jonah's message was well received by the king and the people of Nineveh. They all repented and Nineveh received a stay of execution. Jonah 3:10 says,

> "Then God saw their works, that they turned from their
> evil way; and God relented from the disaster that He had
> said He would bring upon them, and He did not do it."

Is it possible that this historical example could be repeated in America? Could America receive a similar pardon from the Lord? The answer is absolutely, but the Lord does not issue *"get out of jail free"* cards like in the game of Monopoly. America, and its leaders, must repent in order for the Lord to relent from destroying the nation.

Is America having a Jeremiah 7:16 moment?

A nation can reach a point of no return, when the Lord determines that its destruction cannot be averted. This happened to the Southern Kingdom of Judah about 2700 years ago during the time of the Hebrew prophet Jeremiah. Three times he was told not to waste time praying for the people of Judah.[20]

> "Therefore do not pray for this people, nor lift up a cry
> or prayer for them, nor make intercession to Me; for I
> will not hear you. Do you not see what they do in the
> cities of Judah and in the streets of Jerusalem?"

> — Jeremiah 7:16

After Jeremiah received his instruction not to pray for the people of Judah, he forewarned them of their forthcoming judgment. The people would be deported for seventy years into Babylonian captivity and the land would remain desolate during that period.[21]

In His foreknowledge, the Lord knew that Judah would not have a Nineveh or 2 Chronicles 7:14 moment. If Judah would have repented, the Lord would certainly have relented from judgment. The question for Americans to ask is; does America have a national repentance forthcoming in the near future? Only God, who knows the end from the beginning, knows![22]

Is America approaching a Hosea 4:6 moment?

If America, like Judah, has passed the point of no return and has no national repentance in store for its future, then Americans need to prepare for a Hosea 4:6 moment. Hosea warned the Northern Kingdom of Israel that it would be destroyed. This destruction was caused by the Assyrian empire and occurred in 722 B.C.

Hosea urged his fellow Israelites beforehand to become informed so that they could get prepared for the forthcoming destruction. Prophetic information about the destruction of the Northern Kingdom of Israel was abundantly available, not only from his teachings, but also those of the prophets Amos, Isaiah and others. It was not the Lord's fault if His people didn't get the memo.

Hosea 4:1 informs that his message of judgment was for all the inhabitants of Israel, whether they had faith in God or not. Hosea 4:14 warned that everyone, believers and unbelievers, who lacked understanding was going to be trampled, which means those who possessed prophetic awareness could prepare in advance.

Hosea 4:6 says, *"My people are destroyed for lack of knowledge. Because you have rejected knowledge, I also will reject you..."* Since the terrorist attacks of September 11, 2001, the Lord has been warning Americans about the dangers that lie ahead, but are they rejecting those warnings? If so, then as Hosea says, the Lord will reject them.

Learn the Prophetic Word of God

It's high time that Christians sink their teeth into the imminent prophecies of the Bible. They need to understand them and then ask the Lord for protection, direction and opportunities to share the knowledge they glean from this process with others. It is knowledge that will help the people of God through the coming chaos. This knowledge is found in the prophetic word of God.

The Lord foreknew that the final generation would need lots of relevant information in order to live intelligent lives during the turbulent end times. As such, He imparted a plethora of prophetic knowledge ages ago through Christ, the apostles and the Hebrew prophets. This is where believers have to start. They need the information that was intended to equip them for the days in which they live. If this is the final generation, there is more written in the Bible about it than any other generation throughout history.

Don't look for the Lord to lift up some political super hero, rather look to the Lord to lift up HIS HOLY PROPHETIC WORD for your equipping and evangelizing!

Now more than ever before in America, the primary individual focus needs to be on a personal relationship with Christ, rather than on any of the current political leadership. Perhaps the Lord will lift a political hero up inside America, but I'm concerned that as a nation we have arrived at the Jeremiah 7:16 point now. This implies that we need to prepare for a Hosea 4:6 moment.

8

Is America In Ezekiel 38?

This is where we put the prophetic pedal to the metal. If the USA is written about in the Ezekiel 38 prophecy then the ramifications for the future of America are staggering! This chapter unpacks Ezekiel 38:13 to unmask the mysterious modern day identity of ancient Tarshish and their young lions, or "villages" in some translations. Additionally, the role of the young lions in this prophecy will be examined.

Ezekiel 38 and 39 involves at least fourteen participants in the prophecy. They are;

1. *The Victor*: God.
2. *The (intended) Victim*: Israel.
3. *The Invaders*: Magog, Meshech, Tubal, Persia, Ethiopia, Libya, Gomer, and Togarmah. (Refer to the Ezekiel 38 map image to find out the modern day equivalents).
4. *The Protestors:* Sheba, Dedan, the merchants of Tarshish and their Young Lions.

The prophecy informs that, in the latter years the invaders will attack Israel to capture plunder and booty. They covet Israel's economic prosperity and conspire militarily to confiscate this livelihood as part of their spoils of war. As the victor, the Lord prevents this from occurring by utilizing supernatural means to defeat these invaders. Meanwhile, as the epic event unfolds, the protestors complain about the evil intentions of the invaders. Their protests are lodged in the questions in Ezekiel 38:13 quoted below. Ultimately, after the invaders are conquered, Israel graduates from being the intended victim and instead becomes the resultant benefactor.

"Sheba, Dedan, the merchants of Tarshish, and all
their young lions will say to you, 'Have you come to
take plunder? Have you gathered your army to take
booty, to carry away silver and gold, to take away
livestock and goods, to take great plunder?'"

— Ezekiel 38:13

The modern day equivalents of these protestors today are commonly understood and taught to be;

1. *Sheba*: Yemen.
2. *Dedan*: Saudi Arabia and perhaps parts of the Gulf
   Cooperative Council (GCC) Arab Gulf States.
3. *Tarshish*: Either the UK or Spain.
4. *Young Lions*: Either the colonies that came from
   the UK, namely North America, or the offshoots of
   Spain, mainly the Latin American countries.

Ezekiel 38:13 imparts several important clues to the reader.
One of them is that the merchants (of Tarshish) are concerned
about the motives of the invaders. They are not referred to as soldiers, politicians, athletes, entertainers, etc., but as merchants. The
Hebrew word used by Ezekiel is clearly talking about commerce.
Being labeled as merchants in Ezekiel 38:13 insinuates that at least
some of the protestors have commercial interests at stake within Israel at the time of the Magog invasion. This is not a new phenomenon. According to Ezekiel 27:12, Tarshish has been conducting
foreign trade in the Middle East for centuries.

These merchants appear distraught over the possibilities of the
invaders seizing Israel's national assets. This raises the questions, "If
they are concerned about protecting their foreign trade relations
within Israel, why do they not appear to be fighting alongside the
Jewish state in this conflict? Why don't they coalesce militarily to
oppose the Magog coalition?" In 1990, George H. Bush had no
problem assembling an alliance of nations against Saddam Hus-

sein's Iraq in Operation Desert Storm. That American led coalition was comprised of several Arab states, including Saudi Arabia, who is represented as Dedan in Ezekiel 38:13. However, in the Ezekiel invasion, a Desert Storm scenario does not seem to be repeated.

This might mean that passive political leadership is in place, but more likely implies that the protestors lack military prowess at the time. Maybe, these abstaining countries are concerned that their forces won't match up against the invading armies. This is the possible conclusion that I favor.

Who was Tarshish?

According to the Table of Nations in Genesis 10, Tarshish was Noah's great grandson through his son Japheth, who fathered Javan, who in turn fathered Tarshish.

> "And the sons of Javan: Elishah, and Tarshish, Kittim, and Dodanim. Of these were the isles of the nations divided in their lands, every one after his tongue, after their families, in their nations."

> — Genesis 10:4-5, ASV

Where was Tarshish?

The two most favored locations for Tarshish among historians, archaeologists and Bible teachers are Spain or Britain. My research leads me to conclude that Britain is the location of "Tarshish" and the North American countries most resemble their "young lions."

Tarshish settled in the isles or in some translations the coastlands. In addition to the verse above, the theme of Tarshish in connection with the isles shows up in Psalm 72:10, and Isaiah 23:6, 60:9, 66:19. A careful reading of these verses uncovers a clear connection between Tarshish and a geographical location associated with isles or coastlands. One example is below.

"The kings of Tarshish and of the isles shall render trib-
ute: The kings of Sheba and Seba shall offer gifts."

— Psalm 72:10

The isles alluded to could be the British Isles, which are a
group of oversized islands off the northwestern coast of continental Europe that consist of the islands of Great Britain, Ireland and
over six thousand smaller isles.[23]

Many of the maps that display the location of ancient Tarshish
locate it around or beyond the Strait of Gibraltar. The Strait of Gibraltar is the westernmost part of the Mediterranean Sea before it merges
with the Atlantic Ocean. It is the water barrier that separates Southern
Spain from Northern Morocco. It is far to the west of Israel, which is
also a point made in Psalm 48:7. The Psalm says, "*As when* You break
the ships of Tarshish With an east wind." This implies that the ships
are coming to the Middle East from the west, rather than the east.

Bible prophecy expert Dr. Mark Hitchcock points out a possible connection between Tarshish and Britain in his book entitled,
"*The Late Great United States.*" Hitchcock states;

"Some archeologists believe that Tarshish was the ancient name of Britain. "Tarshish" can also mean "beyond Gibraltar" depending on your translation. Tarshish and her villages or young lions — in other words Britain which then settled Canada and the United States and Australia."[24]

Dr. J. R. Church, the founder of Prophecy in the News, says the following about Tarshish in his book called, *"The Guardians of the Grail."*

"An inscription discovered in 1780, on a cliff above Mt. Hope Bay in Bristol, Rhode Island, contained an engraving written in Tartessian Punic. It read: "Voyagers from Tarshish this stone proclaims." The story of the discovery was published in "Reader's Digest," February, 1977. The inscription was believed to have been inscribed around 533 B.C. Harvard University's Department of Archaeology has found five locations within the continental United States where the merchants of Tarshish had colonies."[25]

Another respected Bible prophecy expert that advocates this same connection is Dr. David Hocking, of Hope for Today Ministries. We shared a speaking platform together on July 3, 2011. During that event, Dr. Hocking provided several sound biblical, historical and archaeological reasons that support America as the Young Lions of Tarshish. Dr. Hocking's conclusion that he gave at the event is quoted below. You can watch this entire event at this website: https://vimeo.com/26460214

"If you ask me today if the USA is in Bible prophecy, I would have to say on the basis of historical documentation and on the basis of the British museum and all of its records around Glastonbury that it begins with Great Britain (Tarshish), and undoubtedly as a seed-bearing people it refers to the USA as the "Young Lions."

The founder of Calvary Chapel Costa Mesa, pastor and Bible prophecy teacher Chuck Smith, likewise connects Tarshish with England. Pastor Chuck Smith says;

"Tarshish is England. The young lions could conceivably be the United States, Canada, and Australia."[26]

What was Tarshish famous for?

Tarshish's claim to historical fame was primarily two-fold. *First,* they were known for their vast wealth and abundant mineral resources. We glean this from historical accounts and several Scriptures. One relevant verse is quoted below.

> "Tarshish *was* your (Tyre, a territory in Lebanon) merchant because of your many luxury goods. They gave you silver, iron, tin, and lead for your goods"
>
> — Ezekiel 27:12; *emphasis added*

About 587 BC, Ezekiel acknowledged that "tin" was among the primary metals that came from Tarshish. Cornwall, a county on England's rugged southwestern tip, was the only major source of tin in Europe for the past 2,500 years. In the 19th century there were 400 mines in Cornwall employing 18,000 people. The last mine closed in 2004. It is also true that the mountains of Wales, just north of Cornwall, have been a source of all the minerals and metals listed above in Ezekiel 27:12.[27]

Second, Tarshish gained renown for their extremely sturdy ships. These seaworthy vessels would take extended voyages to transport their exports and imports across the Atlantic Ocean and the Mediterranean Sea. These ships of Tarshish are alluded to at least nine times in the Bible.

> "The ships of Tarshish were carriers of your (Tyre's) merchandise. You were filled and very glorious in the midst of the seas."
>
> — Ezekiel 27:25; *emphasis added*

What About Tarshish Today?

Ezekiel 38:8, 16 notifies that this is a prophecy that finds fulfillment in the last days. Ezekiel 38:13 places Tarshish in the epic event. Since these appear to be the last days, then it's safe to say that ancient Tarshish has a modern day equivalent. This logical deduction applies geographically in the world, and geo-politically in the Middle East. Furthermore, Tarshish and their young lions have a relationship with Israel in this prophecy. This beckons the questions, what nation or nations have played instrumental roles in modernity in the Mideast? What countries have been interacting with Israel the most since its rebirth in 1948?

This seemingly rules out Spain as Tarshish and the Latin American countries as the young lions. The Spanish Empire was a dominant world influence in between the late 15th century until the early 19th century. During that time, Spain shared the global power struggle with the Ottoman Empire, which controlled the Middle East between 1517-1917. Today, both empires have faded from their former glories and neither has much influence in the geo-political affairs of the Middle East in general and Israel specifically.

Around the end of the 18th century, the second rise of the British Empire began. At its height it was considered the largest empire in history. No other nation in history created as many colonies (young lions).[28] The empire grew so rapidly that it became characterized by the phrase, "*the empire on which the sun never set.*" By 1922, the British Empire held sway over about 458 million people, one-fifth of the world's population. Moreover, the empire covered more than 13,000,000 square miles, almost a quarter of the Earth's total land area.[29]

The Ottoman Empire's control over the Middle East ended with its defeat in World War I. Subsequently, Britain and France took sovereignty over the territory. When Israel was rebirthed in 1948, it was Britain, rather than Spain, that controlled the subject territory, which at the time was called Palestine.

Presently, America, not Latin America, is playing a young lion's role in the Mideast. In 1979, the USA was instrumental in brokering a peace deal between Israel and Egypt with President Jimmy Carter, and again in 1994 with Israel and Jordan by President Bill Clinton. It seems as though today, Britain, as Tarshish, is now playing a subservient role behind the young lions of America in important geo-political issues of interest to Israel. On the other hand, Spain and the Latin American countries are not involved much at all in Mideast matters.

Conclusion

I am convinced that the majority of biblical, historical, archaeological, geographical and geo-political arguments for the identity of Tarshish and their young lions favor Britain and America. My conclusions are also based upon a thorough examination of several respectable commentaries that clumsily attempted to connect Tarshish to Spain. In my estimation, the arguments I uncovered in favor of Spain were easily refutable. For more information in this regard, I recommend reading the article called "Tarshish – Britain or Spain."[30]

However, please don't solely take my word for the conclusions drawn in this chapter. Although my findings are biblically based, they do involve some logic, deductive reasoning and speculation. Be like the Bereans in Acts 17:11 that used God's Word to draw their own determinations.

> "These (Bereans) were more fair-minded than those in Thessalonica, in that they received the word with all readiness, and searched the Scriptures daily *to find out* whether these things were so."
>
> — Acts 17:11; emphasis added

If Britain and the USA are mentioned as mere protestors in Ezekiel 38:13, then this should trouble Americans. Why does the greatest superpower that ever existed seem to abstain from fighting alongside Israel at this critical point in its future? We are presently Israel's greatest ally!

The USA, in the past, has consistently voted pro-Israel in the United Nations, even when it was unpopular to do so. We provide Israel with state of the art weaponry and other forms of foreign aid. As of June 15, 2015, Israel is the largest cumulative recipient of U.S. foreign assistance since World War II. To date, the United States has provided Israel $124.3 billion in bilateral assistance.

Why does the USA seem content to remain on the sidelines when Russia and its hordes invade Israel? Is it because America declines from superpower status between now and Ezekiel 38? Great Britain already has! In only seventy years, between 1920 and 1990, in the midst of Israel's rebirthing process, Britain collapsed as a world superpower. Now the sun always sets on the British Empire. Today the UK only spans 94,058 square miles and has a population of only about 64 million.

It's easy to see why Britain, as Tarshish in the prophecy, would tremble at the thought of fighting against the Magog coalition. But what about the USA? Is America following in Britain's same failed footsteps? Will America turn its back on God and Israel, like Britain did when it failed to enact the Balfour Declaration, which was drafted in 1917? Britain's failure to provide territory for a Jewish State at the time led to the extermination of approximately 6 million Jews in World War II!

Will America's decades long push to divide the land of Israel into two states have the same consequences? Is this type of anti-biblical geo-political behavior one of the reasons that America is portrayed as cowardly young lions in Ezekiel 38:13? Joel 3:2 says that one of the reasons God judges the nations is for dividing his land. In modernity, America is at the helm of attempting to divide God's land.

This chapter, along with the prior two concerning America, will hopefully encourage American readers to prepare for the strong possibility that their country is headed for a potentially steep and severe decline!

9

Ezekiel 38:
The Marquee Event

The Ezekiel 38 invasion is the marquee event through which the Lord officially notifies the world that He is the one true God. By way of constant reminder, the key verses in this regard are;

"So I will make My holy name known in the midst of My people Israel, and I will not *let them* profane My holy name anymore. Then the nations shall know that *I am* the LORD, the Holy One in Israel. Surely it is coming, and it shall be done," says the Lord GOD. "This is the day of which I have spoken.""

— Ezekiel 39:7-8

This chapter asks and answers a few important questions concerning this epic episode. For instance;

- Why does the Lord choose the Magog invasion, rather than the Rapture, to uphold His holy name?
- Why does God choose My people Israel, rather than the Church, to do this?
- What does upholding His holy name imply?
- Why is it important for God to uphold His holy name?
- Why does the Lord choose to uphold His holy name in the end times?
- When will Ezekiel 39:7 find fulfillment?
- What are the conditions in Israel before the Gog of Magog invasion?
- What are the conditions in Israel during the invasion?
- What are the conditions in Israel in the aftermath?

Hopefully, the answers provided for these questions will stimulate you to consider the incredible importance of this prophecy. Process the potential ramifications of this marquee event in your own thoughts and prayers. Take the quiet time to allow the Holy Spirit to provide you with additional insights; epiphanies that are not even penned below. Remember, the Lord has specifically selected this event, above all others, to showcase His holiness. Prayerfully beseech Him to provide us with the answers.

Why does the Lord choose the Magog invasion?

One important question is, *"Why does the Lord choose the Gog of Magog invasion, rather than the Rapture, to uphold His holy name?"* For those unfamiliar with the Rapture, it is explained in greater detail in the chapter entitled, *"The Vanishing of the Christians."*

The Rapture is an incredible supernatural event. It involves the instantaneous disappearances, without any warnings, of millions of true believing Christians throughout the world. It is the special occasion when Christ, as the Bridegroom, comes to fetch His bride the Christian Church.

The event is predicted in 1 Corinthians 15:51-53 and 1 Thessalonians 4:15-18. These verses provide enough details so that when the epic episode happens there can be little doubt about what occurred.

Due to the magnitude of the event, it could easily qualify as a candidate prophecy through which the Lord could uphold His holy name. The fingerprints of God will be conspicuously visible all over the miraculous experience. However, the fetching of the Bride by Christ, the Son of God, is not the appropriate time for the Heavenly Father to showcase His divine attributes.

Indulge me to provide you with a personal example to stress this point. On August 10, 2002, I was the best man at my oldest son's wedding. It was a wonderful occasion. The ceremony was pastored by the father of the bride. The customized wedding invitations had the groom and bride's names and all the other pertinent wedding information printed on them. The elegant decorations adorning the reception hall were specifically selected to reflect the theme of that special occasion.

At the time, I owned a successful mortgage company and the father of the bride pastored a church. The event was well attended and pastor Dave and I could have easily plugged our respective workplaces before a very captive audience. However, at no time during the wedding service did Pastor Dave blurt out, "*By the way, come to my church next Sunday, we would love to have you.*" Nor, during the traditional best man's toast to the couple, did I give a shout out to "*Unistate Funding,*" which was the name of my former corporation. Suffice it to say; neither Pastor Dave nor I used the wedding invitations or reception decorations to promote our personal business interests.

Weddings and engagements are designed for the sole purpose of celebrating the union between the bridegroom and the bride. They are special occasions that need no distractions. Even more so, the Rapture is a sacred event for the Son of God. Jesus has been patiently waiting to fetch His bride for about 2000 years now. He is going to whisk her away in the sudden blink of an eye, which emphasizes how much He longs for her. When He comes to catch His bride up into the clouds and carry her over the threshold of heaven's door it will be without delay, not even a single second can separate them.

The reasoning above is one possibility why the Lord chooses the Gog of Magog invasion, instead of the Rapture, to uphold His holy name. Notwithstanding, the Rapture, when it happens, will provide undeniable proof to the people that are left behind, that the God of the Bible, is indeed, the one true God! The people left behind will include those people who may know *a* false god, or who know *of* the true God, but who did not believe in the name of the only begotten Son of God. (John 3:18, 36)

Why does God choose "My people Israel" to uphold His holy name through?

Another relevant question is, *"Why does God choose "My people Israel," rather than the Christian Church, to uphold His holy name?"* One explanation could be, because when the time comes to uphold His holy name, the Christians may have already been Raptured. This possibility is further explored in the chapter called, "Ezekiel 38: The Israeli Perspective."

The choice to use Israel instead of the Church in this important spiritual matter presents a dilemma for replacement theologians. They believe that God is done with the Jews. In essence, the Jews and the nation of Israel are no longer prophetically relevant from their perspectives.

In a nutshell, replacement theologians teach that when the Jews rejected Jesus, God in turn rejected the Jews. This means that the unfulfilled biblical promises to the Jews, and prophecies involving the Jews, have been reassigned in their principle applications to the Christian Church. Yet, Ezekiel 39:7-8 blatantly contradicts this reasoning!

The prophecies in Ezekiel 38 and 39 are specific to the Jews and the land of Israel. These prophecies have not happened, which means unequivocally that God cannot be done with either the Jews or Israel. God keeps His word, and as such, He fully intends to fulfill all of His unconditional covenants and promises! In fact, this is a primary reason that He elects to uphold His holy name through "My people Israel."

God is a Covenant Keeper

The covenant that God made with Abraham approximately 4000 years ago was unconditional and has not found final fulfillment. This means that it is still fully functional. The Lord told Abraham that He would bless him with a "great nation," and that every foreign power would be treated in the same way that they treated Abraham.

> "I will make you a great nation; I will bless you
> And make your name great; And you shall be a
> blessing. I will bless those who bless you, And I will
> curse him who curses you; And in you all the families
> of the earth shall be blessed."

— Genesis 12:2-3

This covenant was confirmed unconditionally in Genesis 15, which means that the Lord took full responsibility for its fulfillment. Even though it's commonly referred to as the Abrahamic Covenant, Abraham had nothing to do with its confirmation. As a matter of fact, Genesis 15:12 says that he was in a deep sleep when the covenant was ratified unilaterally by the Lord.

Genesis 12:3 promised that through Abraham all of the families of the earth would be blessed. Genesis 22:18, 26:4 and 28:14 explain that the unconditional covenant passed on through Abraham's son Isaac and grandson Jacob. These verses also clarify that through their lineage a "Seed" would come. Moreover, the blessings to the families of the earth would come through that "Seed." Tracing Abraham's genealogy through the biblical narrative in Matthew 1:1-16 leads to the inescapable conclusion that Jesus Christ is the "Seed" spoken of.

This means that the unconditional Abrahamic Covenant is pertaining to God's plan for mankind's redemption through Jesus Christ as the Messiah, Who would come through God's covenant people the Jews. This is why the Lord must uphold His holy name through the descendants of Abraham, My people Israel.

Here's how this finds application through My people Israel. The Lord promised to make Abraham a great nation. A great nation requires a land and a people to populate it. Henceforth from that time forward, the terms "Promised Land" and "Chosen People" have characterized the land of Israel and the Jewish people.

According to the Bible, the covenantal promises to Abraham, Isaac and Jacob are eternal. They were promised a land and descendants forever. This is why all historical genocidal attempts against the Jewish people and attempts to permanently take over the land of Israel have failed.

The Lord's covenant keeping character is at stake in the Ezekiel 38 prophecy. The Gog of Magog invaders want to eliminate the Chosen People and possess the bounty of the Promised Land. The prophecy could only find fulfillment when both facets of the covenant were in place. The Ezekiel invaders could never war against the Jews in Israel, if the Ottoman Empire still possessed the subject land and if Hitler had killed all the Jews.

The Lord will defeat the Ezekiel invaders and the Promised Land and Chosen People will survive the massive conflict. The world will marvel when the enemy is decisively defeated through supernatural means. God will be able to say without reservation, that He is the covenant keeping God of Abraham, Isaac and Jacob. This means that He will have upheld His holy name through "My people Israel."

The Lord will also be able to declare through this event that He is the promise keeping God Who sent His only begotten son, Jesus Christ, as a sacrifice for the sins of the world. You might be asking, how so? Perhaps you can accept the conclusion that the Lord is a covenant keeper, but what's Jesus Christ got to do with the Chosen People and the Promised Land?

The Lord is a Promise Keeper

The answer is that the unconditional Abrahamic Covenant does no good for a Promised Land and a Chosen People unless it is governed by a good and perfect king. Included in the Abrahamic Covenant are the Davidic and New Covenants. These are amplifications of the Abrahamic Covenant. The Davidic covenant promises an eternal King in 2 Samuel. The New Covenant makes provisions for the eternal law of forgiveness and a changed heart in Jeremiah 31:31-34.

Davidic Covenant

"When your days are fulfilled and you rest with your fathers, I will set up your seed after you, who will come from your body, and I will establish his kingdom. He shall build a house for My name, and I will establish the throne of his kingdom forever."

— 2 Samuel 7:12-13

New Covenant

"But this *is* the covenant that I will make with the house of Israel after those days, says the LORD: I will put My law in their minds, and write it on their hearts; and I will be their God, and they shall be My people. No more shall every man teach his neighbor, and every man his brother, saying, 'Know the LORD,' for they all shall know Me, from the least of them to the greatest of them, says the LORD. For I will forgive their iniquity, and their sin I will remember no more."

— Jeremiah 31:33-34

Christ is the eternal King!

"He (Jesus Christ) will be great, and will be called the Son of the Highest; and the Lord God will give Him the throne of His father David. And He will reign over the house of Jacob forever, and of His kingdom there will be no end."

— Luke 1:32-33; *emphasis added*

The Holy Spirit is responsible for the implementation of the eternal law. He is the Helper that inscribes the New Covenant on the hearts and minds of believers. He accomplishes this by indwelling the believers. Only through this miraculous feat can the New Covenant be accomplished. Believing Gentiles as *adopted* children of God are grafted into the Abrahamic Covenant through the New Covenant provision. This is the point made by the apostle Paul in Romans 11:11-31.

> "And I will pray the Father, and He will give you another Helper, that He may abide with you forever—the (Holy) Spirit of truth, whom the world cannot receive, because it neither sees Him nor knows Him; but you know Him, for He dwells with you and will be in you."
>
> — John 14:16 -17; *emphasis added*

> "But the Helper, the Holy Spirit, whom the Father will send in My name, He will teach you all things, and bring to your remembrance all things that I said to you."
>
> — John 14:26

The Promise Keeping attribute of God is critically important for all believers because individual salvation is totally dependent upon the Lord honoring His commitments in Ephesians.

> "For by grace you have been saved through faith, and that not of yourselves; *it is* the gift of God, not of works, lest anyone should boast."
>
> — Ephesians 2:8-9

Individual salvation is a gift of grace from God. It is given to us for placing our faith in Christ as our Lord and Savior. It is not something we have achieved through good works. It's available to us only through the completed work that Christ did upon the cross. By upholding His holy name through *My people Israel*, the Lord also demonstrates to everyone who puts their faith in Christ that He will fulfill His covenants and promises to them.

What does upholding His holy name imply?

Ezekiel 39:7 says that the Lord will make His holy name known and not allow it to be profaned anymore. This implies that the Lord is upholding His holy name. To uphold means to confirm or support something that has been questioned. It is the process of defending an established fact.

Moreover, to uphold a truth is to reconfirm its reality, rather than to establish its existence. Long ago in Leviticus 22:32 and elsewhere, the Lord established the fact that His name was holy, and at no time since has He allowed it to be compromised. Thus, there is also need to either establish or re-establish His holiness.

Since the Lord was, is and will always be holy, then what compels Him to reconfirm this in Ezekiel 39:7? There are three primary reasons for this. *First,* His holy name has been severely profaned. *Second,* it has been mostly forgotten. *Third,* it is no longer considered the name above all names in most of the world.

How has the Lord's holy name been severely profaned?

Ezekiel 39:7 says that *"I will not let them profane My holy name anymore."* This alludes to the Jewish people. Ezekiel 36 explains how this happened.

> "Moreover the word of the LORD came to me, saying: "Son of man, when the house of Israel dwelt in their own land, they defiled it by their own ways and deeds; to Me their way was like the uncleanness of a woman in her customary impurity. Therefore I poured out My fury on them for the blood they had shed on the land, and for their

idols *with which* they had defiled it. So I scattered them among the nations, and they were dispersed throughout the countries; I judged them according to their ways and their deeds. When they came to the nations, wherever they went, they profaned My holy name—when they said of them, 'These *are* the people of the LORD, *and* yet they have gone out of His land.' But I had concern for My holy name, which the house of Israel had profaned among the nations wherever they went."

— Ezekiel 36:16-21

These Scriptures inform that the Jews had upset the Lord, which provoked Him to chasten them. This chastening resulted in a national dispersion out of Israel into the nations of the world. This represents what occurred during the Jewish diaspora between 70-1948 A.D.

During the diaspora, the nations misperceived that the God of the Jews was an inept deity that was unable to protect and preserve His people inside their historic homeland. The Gentile countries misconstrued what was happening during the diaspora and the Jews did nothing collectively to correct their thinking. Furthermore, rather than learn their lessons and glorify the Lord, the Jews attempted to assimilate within the nations in a blatant disregard for God.

This behavior defamed God's holy name. The Jews were a chosen people that were set apart by God from the Gentiles. This is the point of Deuteronomy 7:6-8 and Ezekiel 20:32. Even though the Jews were being disciplined within the Gentile nations, they were to remain set apart for God.

"For you (Jews) *are* a holy people to the LORD your God; the LORD your God has chosen you to be a people for Himself, a special treasure above all the peoples on the face of the earth. The LORD did not set His love on you nor choose you because you were more in number than any other people, for you were the

least of all peoples; but because the LORD loves you,
and because He would keep the oath which He swore
to your fathers, the LORD has brought you out with
a mighty hand, and redeemed you from the house of
bondage, from the hand of Pharaoh king of Egypt."

— Deuteronomy 7:6-8

"What you have in your mind shall never be, when you
say, 'We (Jews) will be like the Gentiles, like the families
in other countries, serving wood and stone.'"

— Ezekiel 20:32; *emphasis added*

Ezekiel 36:22-24, in conjunction with Ezekiel 39:7, explains
how the Lord would remedy this problem. These verses inform
that the Jews would return from the nations of the world back into
Israel. This miraculous undertaking would disprove the mistaken
international mindset that the God of the Jews was impotent or in-
competent. Once the regathering was accomplished, then the Lord
could uphold His holy name in the Ezekiel 38 and 39 prophecies.

Why has the Lord's holy name been mostly forgotten?

The 1878 years of Jewish diaspora allowed the nations host-
ing the dispersed Jews to conduct their domestic and international
affairs without any accountability to God's international foreign
policy in Genesis 12:3. This policy was quoted earlier in this chapter. It called for the Gentile nations to bless the Jews in order to be
the recipients of returned national blessings.

The attitude adopted by the nations during the diaspora was,
"Why should we?" Misunderstanding the point of the diaspora,
they saw no value in seeking favor from the God of the Jews. They
conducted their global affairs thinking that they had impunity
from God's commandments. Over time the Lord's holy name was
mostly forgotten.

Due to "Replacement Theology," which plagued Christianity during the diaspora, and is still prominent even today, the Church has by and large failed to reverse this secular mentality. Replacement Theology, which is embraced by Catholics and many mainstream Protestant denominations, echoes the similar world sentiment. They mostly agree with the thinking that the Jews are irrelevant today.

What does the name above all names mean?

The name of God is above all names. He shared this stature with His only begotten son, Jesus Christ.

> "Therefore God also has highly exalted Him and given Him, the name which is above every name, that at the name of Jesus every knee should bow, of those in heaven, and of those on earth, and of those under the earth, and *that* every tongue should confess that Jesus Christ *is* Lord, to the glory of God the Father."
>
> — Philippians 2:9

Elevating the name of Christ was necessary to fulfill the inherent purpose of the Abrahamic Covenant, which was mankind's redemption. Acts 4:12 declares about the name of Jesus that, *"there is no other name under heaven given among men by which we must be saved."*

Why is it important for God to uphold His holy name?

The reason God must uphold His holy name is because man's salvation depends upon it. Only through faith in Christ can one be saved. Over the past 2000 years, the holy name of God has been severely profaned and mostly forgotten. However, God's love for people is as strong today as it was at the time of Adam and Eve. The bottom line is God is not suffering from an identity crisis about His holiness; rather He is going to uphold His holy name for the sake of your salvation. The Lord knows that He is holy, but the question is; DO YOU?

Why did the Lord choose to uphold His holy name in the end times?

The timing and venue selected for God to uphold His holy name was strategic. Possessing the ability to know the end from the beginning, the Lord foreknew the following;

- His name would eventually be severely defamed and mostly forgotten,
- This mentality would be globally prevalent in the end times,
- It would take an epic world event to restore humanities confidence and belief in Him,
- A satanic plan of strong delusion with an Antichrist was forthcoming in the end times,
- This devilish plan of deception would distort the truth about God's holy name,
- Unless God upheld His holy name, humankind would be overwhelmed by Satan's Lie!

God's love for man compelled Him to provide a clear choice in the end times between Christ and the Antichrist. God wishes that everyone would have everlasting life, but this is only available through the holy name above all names of Jesus Christ. 2 Thessalonians 2:9-12 issues an end time prophecy, which predicts that people will perish because they refuse to receive Christ. They make a choice in favor of the Antichrist rather than believing in Jesus Christ. However, their choice to follow this deceiver won't be because the Lord failed to uphold His holy name beforehand.

When will Ezekiel 39:7 find fulfillment?

Ezekiel 39:7 is the marquee event whereby the Lord draws a final red line in the sands of time. He proves Himself before a captive worldwide audience in this major prophetic event. Accreditation for the supernatural defeat of the Gog of Magog invaders will be given exclusively to Him. The reasons for this spectacular episode were previously explained above.

Understanding the Lords declared intentions in Ezekiel 39:7 helps us to understand the timing of this verse's fulfillment. Ezekiel 39:7 must happen sometime before 2 Thessalonians 2:9-12. Upholding His holy name in advance of this 2 Thessalonians prophecy provides ample time for people to make their clear choice for Jesus Christ. After the strong satanic delusion is unleashed in the world, it will be too late.

The Antichrist will utilize this deception to create a system that is designed for people to worship him exclusively. The choice to do so will prompt a person to receive a mark of some specific kind upon their right hand or on their forehead. This is commonly referred to as the "Mark of the Beast." This is described in Revelation 13:14-18. Revelation 14:9-11 says that anyone who worships the Antichrist (Beast) and his image, and takes *his* mark will receive the wrath of God and be tormented forever.

I sincerely doubt that after the Mark of the Beast system is put in place that the Lord's going to slap His forehead and say, *"Oy Vey, I wish I would have upheld my name beforehand; now it's too late!"* No, this is not likely because God is love, (1 John 4:8, 16), and He wishes that none would perish, (John 3:16). The apostle Peter says,

> "The Lord is not slack concerning *His* promise, as some count
> slackness, but is longsuffering toward us, not willing that any
> should perish but that all should come to repentance."

> — 2 Peter 3:9

The other three important questions posed at the beginning of this chapter will be answered in the chapter called, "Ezekiel 38: The Israeli Perspective." By way of review, these questions were;

- What are the conditions in Israel before the Gog of Magog invasion?
- What are the conditions in Israel during the invasion?
- What are the conditions in Israel in the aftermath?

10

Ezekiel 38: The Israeli Perspective

Welcome to the highly anticipated main prophetic event. By the time the Ezekiel 38 prophecy finally arrives, the NOW prophecies should have already laid the ground work for its fulfillment. Israel will likely be responding to, and the world recovering from, the following plethora of prophetic events, (listed below in no specific chronological order);

1. Jeremiah 49:34-39, the Elam prophecy about the disaster in Iran,
2. Isaiah 17 & Jeremiah 49:23-27, the destruction of Damascus,
3. Jeremiah 49:1-6 and Zephaniah 2:8-9, the toppling of Jordan,
4. Isaiah 19:1-18, the terrorization of Egypt,
5. Psalm 83, the concluding Arab-Israeli war,
6. The rebuilding of, or ground breaking for, the third Jewish temple,
7. Obadiah 1:19-20, Jeremiah 49:2 and Zephaniah 2:9, the expansion of Israel,
8. Ezekiel 37:10, 25:14, Obadiah 1:18, the rise of the exceedingly great Israeli army,
9. Ezekiel 38:11, the safer Israel that dwells without partition walls and security fences,
10. Ezekiel 38:13, the wealthier Israel in receipt of great plunder and booty,
11. 1 Corinthians 15:51-53 and 1 Thessalonians 4:15-18, the Rapture of the Church,
12. Ezekiel 38:13, the decline of the UK and USA, (Tarshish and their young lions),

This chapter takes a look at prophecies described in Ezekiel 38 and 39 through the lens of Israel's perspective. The topics covered are:

- What are the conditions in Israel before the Gog of Magog invasion? (Ezekiel 38:1-13).
- What are the conditions in Israel during the invasion? (Ezekiel 38:14-39:8).
- What are the conditions in Israel in the aftermath? (Ezekiel 39:9-21).

The menu of NOW prophecies listed above, which should precede the coming of Ezekiel 38 and 39, are all explored within various chapters of this book. The fulfillment of some or all of these prophecies will dramatically change Israel's current geo-political complexion.

Most contemporary commentaries on Ezekiel 38 approach the prophecy as if it could happen as Israel exists in its present state. However, that is not the perspective presented in this chapter.

Currently, Israel is slightly over 8,000 square miles, which is about the size of New Jersey. It is surrounded by Arab states and terrorist populations that don't recognize Israel's right to exist as the Jewish State. If you believe that Ezekiel 38 finds fulfillment while Israel exists in its current geo-political condition, then how would you answer the following questions?

1. *Why does Russia (Magog) need such a big coalition to invade today's tiny little Israel?* (The list of invaders includes Russia, Turkey, Iran, Libya, Ethiopia, Sudan, Somalia, Morocco, Tunisia, and others). Russia, Turkey, Iran, Tunisia and Libya, not including the other invaders, have populations that currently total over 300 million. When you compare this to Israel's estimated Jewish population of about 6 million, it seems a bit like overkill. Additionally, the Russian army

is ranked #2, the Turkish army is ranked #10 and Iranian army is ranked #23 among world armies. In comparison, Israel is presently ranked #11.[31]

2. *Why doesn't Ezekiel include the Arab states that share common borders with Israel among the Gog of Magog invaders?* After all, these Arabs are the notorious enemies of Israel in the past and still today, but none of the invaders in Ezekiel 38 have ever been historic enemies of Israel. (Excluding perhaps Persia at the time of Esther around 486-468 BC).

3. *Is Israel dwelling securely without walls, bars or gates as per Ezekiel 38:11?* Israel has approximately a 400 mile long wall that runs through much of Israel. In fact, it can be argued that Israel is the most fenced in and fortified country in the world.

4. *Does Israel possess the enormous amount of booty and plunder that the Magog invaders desire as per Ezekiel 38:12-13?* Israel has recently discovered large sources of natural gas, but Russia has no shortage of gas. Most sources place Russia as the #1 supplier in the world of natural gas. Also, Russia is among the top three oil exporting countries in the world.

These are just a few questions, which upon a scrutinous examination, seems to suggest that the Gog of Magog invaders won't coalesce to invade today's Israel. However, if some of the NOW prophecies precede Ezekiel 38, then these same four questions could be answered in this manner;

1. *Why does Russia (Magog) need such a big coalition to invade today's tiny little Israel?*

    Russia needs to formulate a big coalition to invade Israel because;

a. The Israeli Defense Forces (IDF) have become an exceedingly great army in fulfillment of Ezekiel 37:10, 25:14.

b. The IDF accomplished this by decisively defeating the Arabs in Psalm 83, destroying Damascus in Isaiah 17 and toppling Jordan in Jeremiah 49:2.

c. Furthermore, the tiny Jewish state of 2015 has become a significantly larger Israel. This resulted from annexing the formerly occupied Arab lands identified in Obadiah 1:19-20, Zephaniah 2:9, and Jeremiah 49:2.

2. *Why doesn't Ezekiel include the Arab states that share common borders with Israel among the Gog of Magog invaders?*

The Arab states are already defeated by the IDF in fulfillment of the Psalm 83 war.

3. *Is Israel dwelling securely without walls, bars or gates as per Ezekiel 38:11?*

a. Israel is dwelling securely because the IDF has defeated their neighboring enemies. As a result they have militarily, rather than politically, achieved the national security that they had desperately longed for since becoming a nation in 1948.

b. Another possible reason is that they have torn down the partition wall and removed all security checkpoints within the country, after the defeat of their enemies in Psalms 83.

4. *Does Israel possess the enormous amount of booty and plunder that the Magog invaders desire as per Ezekiel 38:12-13?*

Not only has Israel become safer and larger as answered in the three prior questions, but they have also become wealthier. This characteristic is elaborated upon below.

What are the conditions in Israel before the Gog of Magog invasion?

Ezekiel 38:1-13, are the telling verses that describe what Israel looks like geopolitically prior to the Gog of Magog invasion. The biblical text for these verses and all of Ezekiel 38 and 39 is provided in the Appendix entitled; "*The Text of Psalm 83 and Ezekiel 38:1-39:20.*"

Presuming some or all of the NOW Prophecies have occurred; then Israel will be reshaping itself in response to the twelve scenarios presented at the beginning of this chapter. The Jewish state should be understandably *larger, safer* and *wealthier*.

These three conditions should be conducive to an influx of more Jewish aliyah, (Jewish migration into Israel). Jews have been making aliyah into Israel continuously for over a century and this process will likely increase once Israel is freed from the torment of Arab terror. The threat of terror should slow down substantially after Israel defeats its Arab foes in Psalm 83.

Some Jews living outside of Israel are driven to make aliyah to avoid present or perceived future persecution in their present homelands. However, when Israel is *larger* and *safer*, Jews can make aliyah, not only to escape mounting international Anti-Semitism, but also to participate in the expansion of Israel into a *wealthier* nation. The skills and wealth they bring with them could become a contributing factor that leads to the type of prosperous condition described in Ezekiel 38:12-13. These verses portray Israel as possessing a very robust economy.

More land, Jews, economic wealth, military strength and international influence should characterize Israel just before the Gog of Magog invasion. This burgeoning Israel should be bursting at the seams, which will be conducive to improved and expanded foreign relations with other countries. However, this won't be the case for most surviving Muslim nations, like Iran, Turkey, Libya etc. These countries will probably not be pleased with Israel after the fulfillment of several NOW prophecies, like Psalm 83, (Arab-Israeli war), Isaiah 17, (destruction of Damascus), and Jeremiah 49:1-6, (toppling of Jordan).

Leading up to Ezekiel 38, the primary focus of the Muslim nations will be more on the defeat of their fellow Muslims by the IDF, than on the opportunities available to them through this new and improved Israel. Arab casualties of war, prisoners of war and displaced Muslim refugees, will contribute to their hatred toward Israel.

Israel should also be capturing war spoils, which could include increased territory. These spoils of war could be part of the plunder and booty described in Ezekiel 38:12-13. Israel has a pattern of territorial expansion after winning wars. Joshua did this about 3500 years ago. David and Solomon also did this about 3000 years ago. Israel did this in 1967 after the infamous "Six-Day" war.

Israel feels justified in seizing neighboring lands for two primary reasons. *First*, it is part of the land God gave to Abraham in Genesis 15:18. *Second*, because it increases the defensibility of their borders.

The Muslim nations will also be upset with Israel if, after defeating the Arabs of Psalm 83, they break ground on the construction of their third Jewish temple. According to Bible prophecy, Israel will rebuild their temple sometime before the middle of the seven year tribulation period. Today, the Temple Institute in Jerusalem declares that its ultimate goal is, "*To see Israel rebuild the Holy Temple on Mount Moriah in Jerusalem, in accord with the Biblical commandments.*"[32]

Gog's evil plan

Although the surviving Muslim nations should be upset with Israel, and some Western nations supportive of the improved Israel, Russia will be jealous of the thriving Jewish state. A cruel Russian leader surfaces on the scene. In light of Russia's apparent bid to re-emerge as a superpower, some speculate that this ruthless ruler could be Russian President Vladimir Putin. Whoever he is, we are informed in Ezekiel 38:10 that he devises a maniacal plan against Israel.

'Thus says the Lord GOD: "On that day it shall come to pass *that* thoughts will arise in your mind, and you will make an evil plan."

— Ezekiel 38:10

Ezekiel 38:11-13 explains that the Russian leader's "evil plan" is to assemble a formidable strategic coalition in order to invade Israel for the sake of material gain. I point out the tactical aspect of his sinister plan in the chapter entitled "Russia Forms an Evil Plan to Invade Israel," in my book called *Revelation Road, Hope Beyond the Horizon*. The *Revelation Road* chapter posits the possibility that the Magog coalition is strategically assembled by Russia. Certain countries probably coalesce for one or more of the following reasons. Below is a quote from that book.

- *"Predominantly Muslim Nations opposed to Israel* - Apart from Russia, the other countries are predominantly Muslim. They are already spiritually united through their common faith. Although schisms exist between Sunni and Shia nations, they all share a common hatred of Israel. Most of the Ezekiel invaders including, Iran, Libya, Tunisia, Algeria, Morocco, Sudan and Somalia, currently refuse to recognize Israel as the Jewish state.[33]

- *Angry with Israel after Psalm 83* - Presently, these Islamic nations are not fond of Israel. Their disdain toward Israel will increase after the IDF conquers the Muslim confederacy described in Psalm 83.

- *Important Mideast Water Arteries*- The Ezekiel invaders all border the available waterways that Israel will need to export its commerce into world markets. This alignment of nations can blockade these important water arteries. Turkey, Libya, Tunisia and Algeria surround the Mediterranean Sea. Iran can blockade the Persian Gulf. Ethiopia and Somalia can hinder shipments passing through the Red Sea."

The formulation of the evil bent Magog coalition will ruffle more than Israel's feathers. The protestors identified in Ezekiel 38:13 along with other nations that are supportive of Israel will become extremely tense at the time. (*The protestors are identified in the chapter called, "Is America in Ezekiel 38?"*).

All eyes throughout the world will undoubtedly be focused upon the mainstream news channels to see what Russia's evil intentions are. As the Magog coalition takes shape and begins to assemble to the north of Israel, according to Ezekiel 38:6, 15 and 39:2, the onlookers will watch their televisions with bated breath. "*What in the world is Russia up to?*" They will wonder.

As the intent of the invaders becomes perfectly clear, the Muslim nations will mostly applaud or enlist in the coalition. However, the western world will adopt a different attitude. Considering the strong possibility that the Rapture may happen prior to the Ezekiel 38 invasion, the UK, EU and USA will probably be restricted to the role of protestors. The instantaneous unexplained disappearances of the Christians within their populations will present them with an overwhelming dilemma.

On the flip side, if the Rapture has occurred the Muslim nations should be reinvigorated because it will have a lesser impact on these countries than those with a Christian background. The

Rapture involves only true believers, and although many Muslims are currently converting to Christianity, their homelands remain primarily Islamic.

Just when the hordes of Ezekiel 38 invaders are marching upon the soil of Israel, with all their weapons of warfare locked and loaded, something catches them completely off guard! Television viewers around the world become shocked to see that a massive earthquake rocks the area! The sequences of supernatural catastrophes that follow are explained in Ezekiel 38:14-39:8.

What are the conditions in Israel during the invasion?

The previous few paragraphs along with those about to follow in this section are admittedly somewhat speculative. However, author liberties are being taken in order to paint a biblically based portrait of how the Ezekiel 38 invasion might unfold. You are encouraged to have your Bibles open to the pertinent passages to confirm that my interpretations are not too far-fetched.

Ezekiel 38:19-20 says there will be a *"great earthquake in the land of Israel."* The magnitude of the quake will cause all men upon the face of the whole earth to *"shake."* Affected *mountains* will crumble and *walls* will fall. When was the last time you saw mountains, (plural), topple as the result of an earthquake? Also, wonder who might be killed when the affected mountains are thrown down.

Imagine watching this spectacular scene that interrupts the advance of the Magog invaders on your TV set. What is about to follow is all supernatural. Neither the IDF, nor the American military plays any role in what happens next.

Ezekiel 38:21 declares that *"Every man's sword will be against his brother."* This is alluding to the Magog invaders. Apparently, the powerful repercussions from the seismic event causes panic among the troops, who then begin attacking one another. This is not an example of "friendly fire." This is an illustration of what happened in Israel's history when Gideon's 300 man army fought against the Midianites. Judges 7:22 says, "*the LORD set every man's sword against his companion throughout the whole camp.*"

Ezekiel 38:22 informs, "*I will rain down on him, on his troops, and on the many peoples who are with him, flooding rain, great hailstones, fire, and brimstone.*" As if the earthquake, which will topple mountains, crumble walls and result in the killing of one another wasn't enough, matters go from terrible to horrendous for the invaders. Flooding rains accompanied by stone size hailstones pummel the invaders. Fire and brimstone finish them off. By the time all the supernatural events above concludes,

1. The Magog invaders are destroyed,
2. The television watchers around the world are in shock,
3. And, Israel is counting their blessings and praising Jehovah the God of Abraham, Isaac and Jacob.

Ezekiel 39:1-6 provides more graphic details about what happens to the invaders and then Ezekiel 39:7-8 sheds light on the purpose of the experience. These verses have been quoted before in this book, but bear repeating again here.

> "So I will make My holy name known in the midst of My people Israel, and I will not *let them* profane My holy name anymore. Then the nations shall know that *I am* the LORD, the Holy One in Israel. Surely it is coming, and it shall be done," says the Lord GOD. "This *is* the day of which I have spoken."
>
> — Ezekiel 39:7-8

It will be hard for anyone that watched or experienced this event first hand to walk away with any other conclusion than what is said in these two verses.

What are the conditions in Israel in the aftermath?

Ezekiel 39:9-21 explains what happens in Israel in the aftermath of God's supernatural victory over the Magog invaders.

Israel uses the enemy's weapons

Ezekiel 39:9-10 clues us in to the types of weaponry the invaders possess. The weapons must be of the sort that Israel will be able to convert into fuel. Ezekiel says that "*they will make fire with them for seven years.*" The picture is of energy provision for the entire nation, rather than a few isolated households. Verse 9 says, "*those who dwell in the cities,*" utilize this converted weapons-grade fuel.

The widespread use and lengthy seven year span suggests that the weapons must be far more sophisticated than wooden bows and arrows, which would undoubtedly only last a short while. I mention this because some expositors today limit the weapons to wooden ones. I doubt nuclear non-proliferation will reduce Russian arsenals to wood between now and then.

These missiles and rockets that are being converted to fuel in Ezekiel 39:9-10 probably include the ABCs of weaponry—atomic, biological, and chemical. We can presume this because these types of weapons already exist inside the arsenals of Russia and some of their cohorts. Additionally, the dead soldiers appear to require Hazmat (Hazardous Materials) teams to assist with their burial according to Ezekiel 39:14-16. The fascinating fact is that whatever the weapons configuration, Israel will possess the technological know-how to convert them into national energy. Today, whether it is cell phones or irrigation techniques, Israel is on the cutting-edge of technological advances.

The Magog invaders intended to use these weapons to dispossess Israel of its booty, which would include its energy resources, but the opposite occurs. Israel converts the enemy weaponry into additional energy sources for themselves, instead of having their energy sources stolen.

Israel buries the Magog invaders

Ezekiel 39:11-16 describes the location of the mass burial grounds of the destroyed armies of Gog. A valley east of what is probably the Dead Sea is renamed the Valley of Hamon Gog, which means the "hordes or multitudes" of Gog, in Hebrew. Why I believe it refers to a valley in modern-day Jordan is explained in the chapter called, "Greater Israel," of my *Psalm 83, The Missing Prophecy Revealed* book.

We also find in Ezekiel 39:11-16 that the Israelis will be burying the dead in order to cleanse the land. This could imply two things. *One*, that the hordes of Gog's dead soldiers are contaminated, which would require a professional quarantined burial. This contamination could come from either the fallout from their atomic, biological and / or chemical weapons, or the deteriorating corpses strewn across the battlefield. *Two*, the Jews are adhering to their ancient Levitical Law according to Numbers 19:11-22 and Deuteronomy 21:1-9. These verses set forth specifications about the appropriate handling of dead bodies lying on the land of Israel.

Ezekiel 39:17-20 is an invitation "to every sort of bird and to every beast of the field" to partake of the sacrificial meal of the "flesh" and "blood" of the invaders. This passage is not for the faint of heart. I remember hearing prophecy expert Joel Rosenberg, teach this topic at a Calvary Chapel Chino Hills prophecy conference, and he brought tears streaming down from my eyes.

Ezekiel 39:21-29 concludes the chapter with a recap of some Jewish history and a promise to the faithful remnant of Israel that the Lord will pour out His spirit upon them in the end. The Holy Spirit will be bestowed to the faithful remnant when they recognize Christ as their Messiah. This is one of the rewards for believing in Jesus Christ. (John 14:16-17, 26, 15:26, 16:7).

Summary

Ezekiel 38 and 39 provides the most important, well explained, and easy to understand prophecies in the Bible. This is because these chapters foretell of the coming marquis event, whereby the Lord upholds His holy name before the watchful eyes of humankind. The event is so epic that the Lord achieves the undivided attention of mankind. Israelis continuing to inhabit their homeland of Israel, after the prophetic wars of Psalm 83 and Ezekiel 38, will provide humanity with ample evidence to recognize that the God of the Bible is the one true God!

The timing of Ezekiel 38 is critical. It occurs in the end times when the Promised Land of Israel hosts the Chosen People (Israelis). The Rapture of the church could occur before, during or after the event. My personal view is that the Ezekiel 38 is a post-Rapture, but Pre-Tribulation (Pre-Trib) event. I non-dogmatically believe that Ezekiel 38 finds fulfillment prior to the implementation of the Antichrist's "Mark of the Beast" campaign in Revelation 13:11-18.

Topics related to the Timing of Ezekiel 38

Below are a few of my reasons for adopting the post-Rapture, but Pre-Trib. view for the timing of Ezekiel 38.

1. *My people Israel* – God calls the Israelis "My people Israel" three times in Ezekiel 38 and 39. (Ezekiel 38:14, 16 and 39:7). This suggests that the true believers within the Church need not be present. This is all about Israel and the Israelis. This is one reason I believe the Rapture could occur before Ezekiel 38 finds fulfillment.

2. *Israel alone is under attack* – The prophecy takes place in Israel and is an attack against Israelis. The Magog invaders *are not* attempting to destroy and plunder the Vatican, any other nation, or any other religious entity

or Christian denomination. If the Church was present on earth during the fulfillment of Ezekiel 38, it would possibly have been included in the attack with Israel, or mentioned among the protestors of Sheba, Dedan, or Tarshish, yet it is nowhere to be found. This is another reason I suspect that the Rapture might occur before Ezekiel 38 does.

3. *Upholding His Holy name* – The fact that the Lord chooses this end time's episode to uphold His holy name suggests that timing is important. Demonstrating His holiness by delivering Israel from the most massive Mideast invasion in all of history up to that point, gives humanity the opportunity to believe in God before being deceived by the Antichrist. The Antichrist becomes a central figure throughout the seven year Tribulation period. He rises to power through great deception according to 2 Thessalonians 2:8-12. A Pre-Trib fulfillment of Ezekiel 38 provides people with a clear choice between believing in the holy promise keeping God of the Bible, or the unholy deceiver, the Antichrist.

4. *Israel burns weapons for seven years* – in addition to the reason above, I hold to the teaching that Ezekiel 39:9-10 presents another clue to the timing of Ezekiel 38 and 39.

"Then those who dwell in the cities of Israel will go out and set on fire and burn the weapons, both the shields and bucklers, the bows and arrows, the javelins and spears; and they will make fires with them for seven years. They will not take wood from the field nor cut down *any* from the forests, because they will make fires with the weapons; and they will plunder those who plundered them, and pillage those who pillaged them," says the Lord GOD.

— Ezekiel 39:9-10

These Ezekiel verses say that Israel will make fires with the enemy's weapons. Israelis appear to utilize these weapons for energy consumption for a period of seven-years. This will be no problem during the peaceful first half of the tribulation, but not likely during the perilous second half, because Jews will be fleeing for their lives, rather than harnessing this energy.

Concerning the separation point between the first and second halves of the Trib-period, Christ warned the Israelis in Matthew 24:15-22 that they should flee for their lives when they witness the "abomination of desolation," because that signaled a period of "Great Tribulation" was coming. This abominable event occurs at the mid-point of the Tribulation period.

> "Therefore when you see the *'abomination of desolation,'* spoken of by Daniel the prophet, standing in the holy place" (whoever reads, let him understand), "then let those who are in Judea flee to the mountains. Let him who is on the housetop not go down to take anything out of his house. And let him who is in the field not go back to get his clothes. But woe to those who are pregnant and to those who are nursing babies in those days! And pray that your flight may not be in winter or on the Sabbath. For then there will be great tribulation, such as has not been since the beginning of the world until this time, no, nor ever shall be. And unless those days were shortened, no flesh would be saved; but for the elect's sake those days will be shortened."

> — Matthew 24:15-22

These Matthew 24 verses are part of the reason the second half of the Tribulation is commonly called the Great Tribulation. It stands to reason that if Christ instructs Israelis to flee immediately for safety at the midpoint of the Tribulation period that the refugees won't be stopping along the way to convert anymore of these weapons in the process. If anything, they might pick up a weapon to use it, rather than burn it.

Therefore, many scholars suggest that Ezekiel 38 and 39 must conclude, not commence, no later than three and one-half years before the seven-years of tribulation even begins. This allows the Jews seven full years to burn the weapons before they begin fleeing for their lives.

11

Psalm 83: The Final Arab-Israeli War

Final Arab-Israeli War

Creation of Israel		EZEKIEL 38
	68 YEARS	Psalms 83
1948	2016	20??

Psalm 83 was authored by Asaph about 3000 years ago. Among Asaph's several spiritual attributes, was the gift of prophecy. He was a prophet according to 2 Chronicles 29:30. 1 Chronicles 25:1-2 informs that Asaph and his sons were specifically instructed by King David of Israel to prophesy. I emphasize Asaph's ability to prophesy because some Bible experts don't consider Psalm 83 to be a prophecy. They treat it simply as an imprecatory prayer, or a prayer of lament.

Asaph wrote 12 of the 150 Psalms. He penned Psalm 50 and Psalms 73-83. Amongst all of these Psalms, Psalm 83 is the most prophetic. The Psalm foretells of a coming Arab alliance that conspires together to eradicate the Jewish state of Israel. This confederacy will be soundly defeated by the IDF. In the aftermath, Israel will achieve the peace and security that has eluded the Jewish state since its recreation in 1948. This IDF victory seems to provide Israel with the peace and security that is predicted in Ezekiel 38:8, 11 and 14.

This chapter treats Psalm 83 as a NOW Prophecy because it appears that Ezekiel 38 and 39 won't happen until Psalm 83 has been fulfilled and this peace has been achieved. The *minor premise* for this conclusion is based upon Israel's present inability to dwell securely in fulfillment of Ezekiel 38:8, 11, and 14. Due to the current instability in the Middle East, Israel lacks the ability to dwell securely. The fulfillment of Psalm 83 should rectify this problem by better stabilizing the region.

The *major premise* is that until Israel dwells securely, Ezekiel 38 and 39 won't happen. Yet, Ezekiel 38 and 39 must happen in order for the Lord to uphold His holy name in fulfillment of Ezekiel 39:7. Therefore, some major event must occur that enables Israel to dwell in peace and safety. Psalm 83 appears to be that significant event.

Some Bible prophecy experts argue that the security spoken of in Ezekiel 38 already exists. They teach that it refers to a relative confidence in the IDF's capabilities to protect Israel from its enemies. Thus, they believe that Israel presently dwells securely in fulfillment of this specific condition. Those who accept this teaching should consider the following comments and related questions.

- As of February, 2014 an estimated 63% of Israelis owned gas masks.[34] That number has likely increased since then. *Do you own a gas mask?*

- Most Israelis know the location of their nearest bomb shelter. *Do you know where your nearest bomb shelter is?*

- Israelis are recommended to reach their bomb shelters within15 seconds to 3 minutes, depending on which city they reside in.[35] *Do you know the recommend evacuation time for your city? Does your city even have a recommendation in this matter?*

- In 2006, some northern Israelis spent about a month in bomb shelters during the Hezbollah – Israel war. *Have you ever spent 5 minutes in a bomb shelter?*

- Hamas has lobbed thousands of missiles into Israel since 2005. They still continue to launch missiles into Israel. *Have you ever had to duck and cover from an incoming missile?*

- Israel has protective walls and security fences inside the country and on all of its land bearing borders. *Is this the similar case in your country?*

- Israel is surrounded by populations that don't recognize the existence of the Jewish state. *Does your country have neighbors sharing common borders that refuse to recognize your countries right to exist?*

- Police cars in Jerusalem drive with their blue lights flashing continuously, even though they are not engaged in an active crime pursuit. This is done to give residents the comfort of knowing that they have law enforcement nearby. *Does your local cop car flash his blue lights continually, even though he's not engaged in an active crime pursuit? If he did, would you thank him, or ask him to please stop because it's unnerving?*

These are just a couple basic comments that imply Israel dwells insecurely, rather than securely. These don't even take into consideration the facts that;

- Iran is building a nuclear weapon and wants to wipe Israel off of the map,

- Hezbollah has an estimated 150,000 advanced missiles pointed at a bank of targets throughout the Jewish state,

- Every known Islamic terrorist group in the Middle East wants to severely harm Israel.

The trend among world leaders today is to pressure Israel to give up precious Promised Land for an elusive peace deal with the Palestinians. These world leaders are ignorant of the fact that the land in question is not going to change hands from the Jews to the Arabs. If my understanding of Bible prophecy is correct, Israel is about to increase, rather than decrease in size.

More, not less, Jews are going to migrate to Israel as part of God's plan in fulfillment of several Bible prophecies. This necessitates the expansion, rather than the contraction of the Jewish state. The international community may succeed in forcing Israel to temporarily concede some land, but that won't provide a permanent solution to the Arab-Israeli conflict. Furthermore, any land gains the Arabs achieve prior to Psalm 83, will be returned after Psalm 83.

Psalm 83: The Missing Prophecy Revealed

Before I complete the rest of this chapter, let me draw your attention to my book entitled, *"Psalm 83: The Missing Prophecy Revealed, How Israel Becomes the Next Mideast Superpower."* All the statements made and conclusions drawn within this chapter are based upon the years of research that were poured into the authoring this Psalm 83 book. Therefore, if you have questions, criticisms or need further research, the Psalm 83 book can help in all of those areas.

I apologize in advance if the conclusions presented in this chapter seem authoritative or dogmatic, but I'm attempting to cut right to the point of the prophecy. The Psalm 83 book answers every objection that I have encountered over the years about the Psalm. Every question, comment and criticism concerning Psalm 83 as an unfulfilled Bible prophecy is treated sincerely and objectively within that book.

The Table of Contents of the Psalm 83 book is included in the products section at the end of this book. This was not done to plug the book, but to show the reader the topics covered inside that book if they want to study it in greater depth. This enables me to narrow the focus of this chapter upon the NOW Prophecy aspects of Psalm 83.

Psalm 83 Overview

Psalm 83 is a prophecy about an Arab confederacy that wants to eliminate the Jews from the Jewish state and confiscate the Promised Land of Israel.

> "Do not keep silent, O God! Do not hold Your peace, And do not be still, O God! For behold, Your enemies make a tumult; And those who hate You have lifted up their head. They have taken crafty counsel against Your people, And consulted together against Your sheltered ones. They have said, "Come, and let us cut them off from *being* a nation, That the name of Israel may be remembered no more." For they have consulted together with one consent; They form a confederacy against You. "

> — Psalm 83:1-5

This prophecy is such a big deal that Asaph beseeches the Lord to be very vocal and proactive about this epic event. He pleads, "*Do not keep silent, O God! Do not hold Your peace, And do not be still, O God!*"

The Lord mostly broke His silence in this matter around 2008 when my first book on Psalm 83 came out entitled, "*Isralestine, The Ancient Blueprints of the Future Middle East.*" At the time, Google searches on "Psalm 83 War," or "Psalm 83 Prophecy" netted very few results. However, that's not the case today. Google searches today reveal hundreds of thousands of results. A YouTube video/audio search on January 2, 2016, on Psalm 83 netted 282,000 results. A random sample of about 1000 of these results evidenced that none of them were posted before the 2008 release date of *Isralestine*.

Since then, I have been on most of the top mainstream Christian radio and television shows introducing Psalm 83 to millions of listeners and viewers. Many other widely respected Bible prophecy experts, like Hal Lindsey, Dr. Chuck Missler and Dr. David Reagan are also trumpeting the Psalm 83 prophetic message to the world today.

The prophecy specifies that a group of Israel's enemies confederate and form a devious plan to destroy Israel. *"They have said, "Come, and let us cut them off from being a nation, That the name of Israel may be remembered no more."*

This prophecy did not find fulfillment in the past up to 70 A.D. when Israel formerly existed. It could not have found fulfillment between 70 – 1948 A.D. when Israel no longer existed. However, it can find fulfillment NOW that Israel presently exists!

Psalm 83:6-8 identifies the belligerents by their ancient names.

"The tents of Edom and the Ishmaelites; Moab and the Hagrites; Gebal, Ammon, and Amalek; Philistia with the inhabitants of Tyre; Assyria also has joined with them; They have helped the children of Lot. *Selah"*

The image and map below identify the modern day equivalents of these historical populations.

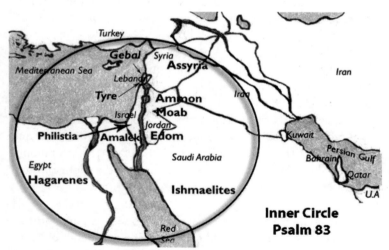

(Map designed by Lani Harmony Salhus of Urban Charm. They picture the ancient names superimposed over their modern day equivalents).

THE PSALM 83 CONFEDERERATES

TENTS OF EDOM	PALESTINIANS & SOUTHERN JORDANIANS
ISHMAELITES	SAUDIS (ISHMAEL FATHER OF ARABS)
MOAB	PALESTINIANS & CENTRAL JORDANIANS
HAGARENES	EGYPTIANS – (HAGAR EGYPT MATRIARCH)
GEBAL	HEZBOLLAH & NORTHERN LEBANESE
AMMON	PALESTINIANS & NORTHERN JORDANIANS
AMALEK	ARABS OF THE SINAI AREA
PHILISTIA	HAMAS OF THE GAZA STRIP
TYRE	HEZBOLLAH & SOUTHERN LEBANESE
ASSYRIA	ISIS & SYRIANS AND NORTHERN IRAQI'S

Notice that the first member listed in the confederacy is the "*tents of Edom.*" This identifies a population in their habitation condition. They appear to be refugees in this prophecy. Presently, the Palestinian refugees have ancient Edomites within their ranks. The Palestinians are a mish-mash of historical peoples, which includes Edomites.

Also duly noted is the fact that the *tents of Edom* are positioned first among the other ten Arab confederates. This implies that they are the star of the Psalm 83 show. Like the credits at the end of movie identify the main stars first, followed by the co-stars second, the Bible often banners the belligerents and their plights in their order of priority.

If Asaph was with us today, I think he would warn us;

> *"When you see the Palestinian refugees and their Arab supporters confederating and conspiring to take the land from Israel away from the Jews, then Psalm 83 is about to find fulfillment."*

The refugees of Palestine became a reality only after Israel became a nation in 1948. Only then did Psalm 83 become prophetically feasible. The Arab states of Psalm 83 are the ones that voted against the creation of Israel at the United Nations in 1947. Furthermore, they warred against Israel in 1948. The ugly byproduct of that war was the creation of refugees of Palestine. Today they are called the Palestinian Refugees. When Asaph predicted their arrival upon the world scene over 3000 years ago, he labeled them as, the *"tents of Edom."*

Presently, these Arabs of Psalm 83 are attempting to dispossess Israel of land politically. However, Psalm 83 predicts they will move against Israel militarily. Psalm 83:12 says, *"Let us take for ourselves the pastures of God for a possession."* This is the declared mandate of the Arab confederacy. They want to possess the Promised Land. The Hebrew word for take is *"yarash."* It can be interpreted in this instance to mean, *to take over* or *to drive out completely.* Thus, Psalm 83:12 could be translated to say, *"Let us drive the Jews out of Israel, so that we can take possession of the Jewish state!"*

If Psalm 83 happens in our time, it means that the majority of Arabs don't desire peace with the Jews. They seek peace without the Jews, meaning NO MORE JEWS! They don't want a two state resolution; rather they demand a single state solution. Simply put, the Psalm 83 plan is to eliminate the Jewish state in order to establish a Palestinian state called Palestine.

The eradication of the Jews and stealing of the land of Israel flies in the face of God's end time's plan to inform the world that He's the one true God. Either God is going to prevail in His endeavor to uphold His holy name through "My people Israel," or He's going to become the laughingstock of all times! Place your wager. Will it be the false god, Allah of the Arabs, or the true God Jehovah of the Jews that prevails? The way I framed the question tells you whom I'm betting on!

The Role of the IDF in Psalm 83

Asaph petitions the Lord in Psalm 83:9-18 to empower the IDF to conquer the Psalm 83 Arab confederacy. His pleadings begin in Psalm 83:9-11. In these verses Asaph calls attention to the historical war examples depicted in Judges 4-8 concerning the Midianites and Canaanites. The Midianites had oppressed the Israelites for seven years and the Canaanites for twenty years. Both peoples were soundly defeated and neither ever oppressed the Jewish people or the land of Israel after their rousing defeats.

Asaph requests a replication of these past war strategies in order to achieve the same results for Psalm 83. In these instances, the IDF was significantly outnumbered, which is also the case today. The Psalm 83 Arab populations presently number about 180 million compared to Israel's meager populace of about 8 million.[36] This means that there are about 22 Psalm 83 Arabs to every 1 Jew. Compare this to Gideon's 300 man army in Judges 7:16, who killed 120,000 Midianite soldiers in Judges 8:10. This was about a 400 to 1 Midianite verses Jew ratio.

In the case of the Gideon military model, the Lord empowered the vastly outnumbered IDF of that time to soundly defeat the Midianites. The conquest included killing the Midianite army and their kings and princes in Judges 7:25 and 8:21. Asaph is asking for the repeat of a similar spectacular scenario. This means the utter defeat of the Psalm 83 armies and their leaders. It requires a severe thrashing that permanently removes all possibilities of a future Arab-Israeli conflict.

Psalm 83 concludes by painting a vivid portrait of what Asaph petitions the Lord for. What he asks for in these passages can only be achieved militarily though conquest, rather than politically through diplomacy.

> "O my God, make them like the whirling dust, Like the chaff before the wind! As the fire burns the woods, And as the flame sets the mountains on fire, So pursue them with Your tempest, And frighten them with Your storm.
> Fill their faces with shame, That they may seek Your name, O LORD. Let them be confounded and dismayed forever; Yes, let them be put to shame and perish."

The Purposes of Psalm 83

The fulfillment of Psalm 83 will accomplish at least eight important purposes, which are;

1. The survival of the Jews in Israel,
2. The maintaining of Jewish control over Jerusalem and all of Israel,
3. Peace and security within Israel, at least until Ezekiel 38 follows,
4. The fulfillment of Ezekiel 37:10 which foretells, that Israel will become an *"exceedingly great army."*
5. The end of all Psalm 83 Arab aggression against Israel,
6. The termination of the ancient Arab hatred of the Jews,
7. The evidence that God's Gentile foreign policy in Genesis 12:3 is still in effect.
8. The proof that the Lord is the one true God. (This is described in Psalm 83:18, which is quoted and explained below).

Purpose #7 will be of paramount importance for the world leaders to acknowledge. If they will learn this important lesson, and apply it in their future interactions with Israel, they can bring blessings upon their respective nations.

The lesson is that God's foreign policy, which was issued about 4000 years ago in Genesis 12:3, is still in fully operational today. The Lord still blesses those who bless Israel and curses them that curse Israel. The Psalm 83 Arabs will make the fatal mistake to curse the Chosen People (Jews) and possess the Promised Land of Israel. These Arabs will be severely cursed as a result!

The ultimate goal of Psalm 83 is number #8 above and is summed up in this concluding verse, *"That they may know that You, whose name alone is the LORD."*

This verse identifies the desired outcome of the IDF conquest over the Psalm 83 Arab confederacy. Some of the Psalm 83 Arab survivors from Jordan, (Jer. 48:47 and 49:6) Egypt, (Isaiah 19:18), and Syria, (Isaiah 19:18) will eventually recognize that the God of the Bible is the one true God. However, apart from the Arabs today that are true followers of Christ, the others are mostly Muslim. They believe Allah is god. The fulfillment of Psalm 83 will prove them wrong!

12

The Destruction Of Damascus

Destruction of Damascus

Creation of Israel	EZEKIEL 38
68 YEARS	ISAIAH 17
1948	2016 20??

Another NOW prophecy at the top of the list involves the destruction of Damascus, Syria. Isaiah 17:1 predicts that Damascus will be utterly destroyed as a city someday. The literal interpretation of the verse reads that the city will be reduced to a ruinous heap of rubble. A few important facts about the city of Damascus are;

- It is thought to be one of the oldest continuously inhabited cities in history, dating back over 4,000 years ago to the time of the Hebrew patriarch Abraham,

- It is the capital city of modern day Syria,

- It is a strategic target for the Israeli Defense Forces (IDF) to attack, and some Israeli leaders in the past have stated that Damascus would be destroyed if Syria ever attacked Israel.[37] In December of 2014, the Syrian military accused Israel of carrying out two air strikes on Syria near Damascus.[38] Subsequently, on November 11, 2015, Syrian media sources reported another Israeli attack upon Damascus.[39]

- It is presently under the control of the government of Bashar Al-Assad, who is loyal to the Iranian government, which was identified in a previous chapter as an enemy of Israel's.

Some Bible prophecy teachers, like Dr. Mark Hitchcock, believe that this prophecy was historically fulfilled by the Assyrian conquest of Damascus in 732 B.C. Concerning the destruction of Damascus according to the Isaiah 17 prophecy, Dr. Hitchcock writes the following in his book called Middle East Burning:

"I believe it makes more sense to hold that Isaiah 17 was fulfilled in the eighth century BC when both Damascus, the capital of Syria, and Samaria, the capital of Israel, were hammered by the Assyrians. In that conquest, both Damascus and Samaria were destroyed, just as Isaiah 17 predicts."[40]

I respectfully disagree with this assessment, and point out that Isaiah mentions Assyria, Assyrian, or Assyrians at least 41 times in his 66 chapters, but never once mentions any of the above in Isaiah 17. To the contrary, Isaiah 17:9 seems to suggest that Israel is responsible for this destruction. The verse states that the desolation is brought about by the "children of Israel." This would allude to the IDF. Isaiah 17:14 informs that the destruction happens overnight and appears to be a retaliatory act in self – defense.

Additionally, Jeremiah 49:23 – 27, which was written more than a century after Isaiah 17, also talks about a burden against Damascus. If Damascus was literally destroyed in 732 B.C. by the Assyrians, this means that it would have had to become restored subsequently for Jeremiah's prophecy to find a future fulfillment. I think it is more logical to read Isaiah 17 and Jeremiah 49:23 -27 in connection with each other to glean more prophetic details of the destruction of Damascus.

Text of Jeremiah 49:23-27

"Against Damascus. "Hamath and Arpad, (Historic
Syrian cities), are shamed, For they have heard bad
news. They are fainthearted; *There is* trouble on the sea;
(Possibly the Mediterranean Sea), It cannot be quiet.
Damascus has grown feeble; She turns to flee, And fear
has seized *her.* Anguish and sorrows have taken her like
a woman in labor. Why is the city of praise, (Jerusalem),
not deserted, the city of My joy? Therefore her young
men, (civilian casualties), shall fall in her streets, And all
the men of war, (military casualties), shall be cut off in
that day," says the LORD of hosts. "I will kindle a fire in
the wall of Damascus, And it shall consume the palaces
of Ben-Hadad, (Syrian governmental buildings).""
(Emphasis has been added in parenthesis).

Summary outline of Jeremiah 49:23-27

The *italicized* words below are quoted from the verses above.

1. *Bad News* befalls Syria, making it become *fainthearted.*
2. The disturbing news is that there is *trouble on the sea.*
3. *It cannot be quiet,* referring to the *trouble on the sea.* This
   could be alluding to lethal missiles launched from the
   Mediterranean Sea on route to Damascus.
4. *Damascus has grown feeble;* the entire city is shaken, probably from the severe missile strikes.
5. Everyone in Damascus panics and *turns to flee. Fear has
   seized* the entire city, *like a woman in labor.*
6. There are many civilian casualties as *young men shall fall
   in* the *streets.*
7. The Syrian army is destroyed as *all the men of war* are *cut off.*
8. *The lord,* as the perpetrator of the attack, *will kindle a fire*
   in Damascus.
9. The governmental buildings are destroyed like in Syrian
   history when *the palaces of Ben Hadad* were *consumed.*

The interpretation of Jeremiah 49:23-27 in correlation with Isaiah 17

Jeremiah 49:23-27 and Isaiah 17 are likely parallel passages of the same prophecy. Each provides separate details that cooperatively intertwine. It would be comparable to having two separate news reporters covering the same event from different camera angles.

Jeremiah doesn't directly tell us who causes the destruction of Damascus, but Isaiah does. He identifies the IDF, (the children of Israel), as the cause of the desolation in Damascus and other fortified Syrian cities.

> "In that day his, (Syria's), strong cities will be as a forsaken bough And an uppermost branch, (including northern cities of Syria), Which they left because of *the children of Israel*; (IDF), And there will be desolation."

— Isaiah 17:9; *emphasis added*

Isaiah informs that strong cities will be forsaken, but apart from Damascus, neglects to specify which ones. Jeremiah provides those details. Jeremiah 49:23 says, *"Hamath and Arpad are shamed."*

Historically, Hamath and Arpad, in addition to Damascus, were among Syria's most notable, (strong), cities. Arpad probably represents Aleppo today, which is Syria's most populated city, and Hamath most resembles the cities of Homs and Hama, which rank as Syria's third and fourth occupied cities. Damascus is the second most inhabited Syrian city. It is important to note that the population demographics are changing in Syria as a result of the Syrian revolution that began in March of 2011.

Strategically speaking, all four cities are on the western side of Syria. They are mostly connected by a single highway that runs north to south. Disrupting traffic to and fro on that critical road would choke off the military and commercial lifeline between

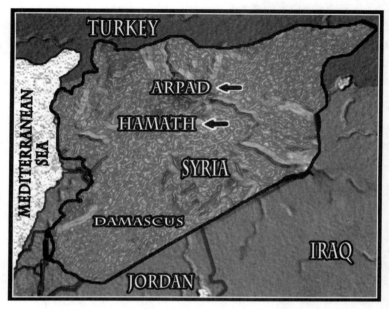

them. It is conceivable that the IDF, the number one ranked army in the Middle East, could isolate and destroy each of these cities.

Isaiah neglects to directly inform whether the IDF attack upon Damascus is by air, land, sea or any of the above. However, Jeremiah 49:23 says that there is *"trouble on the sea; it cannot be quiet."* The Hebrew word is *"deagah,"* which can also be translated as *anxiety, sorrow* or *heavy concern.* In essence, there is sorrow stemming out from some sea. This is the only place in the Scriptures where the adage, *trouble on the sea,* is used. Thus, this is not a colloquialism that tolerates a typological or allegorical explanation; rather it demands a literal interpretation! It foretells of disturbing events occurring within, or coming out from, some sea that will cause heavy sorrows to Syrians!

What sea? What events? These are the logical questions to ask. Considering the severity of the military and civilian casualties predicted in Jeremiah 49:26, one might conclude that missiles launched from some sea results in at least part of the devastation.

The sea is most likely the Mediterranean Sea, which happens to be where several Israeli owned Dolphin class nuclear submarines patrol. These are ships that Israel obtained from Germany. They are capable of launching missiles, potentially nuclear, into the heart of Syria. As a matter of fact, Israel received its fifth Dolphin-class submarine from Germany in January of 2016.[41]

How prolonged is the attack that levels Damascus? Jeremiah 49 says that troubling news causes people to flee from the warzone. This suggests that some Syrians escape into exile. However, Jeremiah 49:26 says, "*young men shall fall in her streets, And all the men of war shall be cut off in that day.*" Does the phrase, "*in that day,*" allude to a 24 hour day? Concerning the length of time, Isaiah informs,

"Then behold, at eventide, trouble! *And* before the morning, he (Damascus) *is* no more. This *is* the portion of
those who plunder us, And the lot of those who rob us."

— Isaiah 17:14; *emphasis added*

Isaiah says, one night you see Damascus, but in the morning it no longer exists. Perhaps, the military conflict between Syria and Israel extends beyond a single day, but in only one night Damascus gets toppled. Israel already possesses the advanced weaponry capable of destroying a major city. This is one of the reasons that the destruction of Damascus is a very viable NOW Prophecy.

Why Damascus? The answer to this question is provided directly by Isaiah and indirectly by Jeremiah. Isaiah 17:14 ends with, "*This is the portion of those who plunder us, And the lot of those who rob us.*" Syria, represented by its capital city, is guilty of plundering and robbing Israel. This appears to be why the IDF wages war against Syria.

Jeremiah 49:25 asks the question, "*Why is the city of praise not deserted, the city of My joy?*" Herein, lays another important clue as to why Damascus gets downed. The praiseworthy city of the Lord's joy is Jerusalem. The question could be asked as follows; "Why is Damascus under attack, while Jerusalem remains intact?"

This implies that Syria's judgment is retaliatory in nature. Something sinister coming from Syria against Jerusalem is likely at issue. Syria, in the process of plundering and robbing Israel, is probably provoking Jews to flee from Jerusalem. Why is Jerusalem not deserted, is the rhetorical question? Jeremiah predicts that Damascus will be deserted, but then inquires, why isn't Jerusalem?

This question makes most sense if there is a conflict taking place between Syria and Israel. If Syria was attacking Saudi Arabia unsuccessfully, then the appropriate question would be, "Why isn't Mecca deserted?"

The curse-for-curse-in-kind clause in Genesis 12:3 finds application in this Syrian-Israeli conflict. This clause determines a like reaction for any foreign power action that affects Israel. If a nation blesses Israel, they will be blessed by the Lord. If they curse Israel, they will be cursed in like manner. Syria wants to harm Israel militarily, so the Lord empowers the IDF to reverse the curse militarily. Syria wants Jews to desert from Jerusalem, so the Lord has Syrians desert from Damascus. Syrians seemingly want to overtake Jerusalem as soon as possible, so in direct retaliation, the Lord has Damascus destroyed overnight.

The destruction of Damascus could be an event that correlates with Psalm 83. Syria participates in Psalm 83:8 under the banner of Assyria. However, when Psalm 83 was written about 3000 years ago, Assyria did not include all of modern-day Syria. It mostly covered parts of northern Syria and northern Iraq. In 732 B.C., the Assyrian Empire took control of Damascus and the rest of what is presently modern day Syria. This means that the destruction of Damascus could occur independently from Psalm 83, because Damascus was not part of Assyria when Asaph authored Psalm 83.

Whether or not Isaiah 17 is part of Psalm 83, both events appear to be NOW Prophecies. This is partially determined by the fact that the IDF participates in each event. The IDF is the tool utilized by the Lord to destroy Damascus, (Isaiah 17:9), and to end the Arab-Israeli conflict, (Psalm 83:9-11). Both prophecies deal with a similar Arab-Israeli scenario.

This ethnic struggle is deeply rooted in an ancient Arab hatred of the Jews. Ezekiel 35:5 and 25:15, are a couple of Scriptures that allude to this adversarial disposition. Some Bible versions translate it as a "perpetual enmity." It is a cancerous condition that must be surgically removed. According to the Bible, it will come to an end, but only when its Arab hosts are soundly and finally defeated.

The body of research that supports these conclusions above is provided in my book called, *"Psalm 83: The Missing Prophecy Revealed, How Israel Becomes the Next Mideast Superpower."* This book also provides a detailed commentary on all of Isaiah 17.

A passing note about today's IDF; they exist today in fulfillment of Bible prophecies in Ezekiel 25:14, 37:10, Obadiah 1:18 and several others. Their primary purpose is to protect and preserve the modern day Jewish state. They are biblically relevant for several NOW prophecies. However, they are not instrumental in the NEXT prophecy of Ezekiel 38 or the LAST prophecy of Armageddon. The Lord stops the Ezekiel 38 invaders and Christ stops the Armageddon campaign of the Antichrist. Neither of those two major events are NOW prophecies.

13

The Trembling And Toppling Of Jordan

Toppling of Jordan

Creation of Israel		EZEKIEL 38
	68 YEARS	Jeremiah 49:1-6
1948	2016	20??

Another ancient Bible prophecy seems to be nearing its fulfillment! The subject nation of this vastly overlooked prediction is Jordan. Approximately 2600 years ago, the Hebrew prophet Jeremiah foretold of a tormenting fear that would someday debilitate and destroy this Arab state.

The prophecy informs that Jordan will tremble as troubling events encroach in on all sides of its borders. Jeremiah 49:5 predicts that terrorizing geo-political events surrounding Jordan will severely destabilize the nation. The terror that Jeremiah describes has never engulfed this territory; *that is until NOW!*

According to Jeremiah 49:1-5, which is quoted below, the instability that occurs within the country burgeons into an epic biblical war against Israel, which results in the,

- Trembling and toppling *of Jordan,*
- Dispersion of Jordanians *from Jordan,*
- Expansion of the Jewish state *into Jordan.*

"Against the Ammonites. (*Northern Jordanians*) Thus says
the LORD: "Has Israel no sons? Has he no heir? Why then
does Milcom (*Pagan god formerly worshipped by the Ammonites*) inherit Gad, (*One of tribal territories belonging to
Israel*) And his people dwell in its cities? Therefore behold,
the days are coming," says the LORD, "That I will cause to
be heard an alarm of war In Rabbah (*Amman, Jordan*) of the
Ammonites; It shall be a desolate mound, (*Toppled*) And her
villages shall be burned with fire. Then Israel shall take possession of his (*Promised Land*) inheritance," says the LORD.
"Wail, O Heshbon, for Ai (*Ancient cities in Northern Jordan*)
is plundered! Cry, you daughters of Rabbah, Gird yourselves
with sackcloth! Lament and run to and fro by the walls; For
Milcom (*False god*) shall go into captivity With his priests
(*Religious leaders*) and his princes (*Political leaders*) together.
Why do you boast in the valleys, Your flowing valley, and O
backsliding daughter? Who trusted in her treasures, saying,
'Who will come against me?' Behold, I will bring fear (*Jordan will tremble*) upon you," Says the Lord GOD of hosts,
"From all those who are around you; You shall be driven
out, (*Exiled from Jordan*) everyone (*Refugees*) headlong, And
no one will gather those who wander off."

— Jeremiah 49:1-5; emphasis added

Is the Trembling and Toppling of Jordan a NOW Prophecy?

In the verses above, Jeremiah asks three rhetorical questions,
which some Jordanian generation will be required to answer. Since
certain details in these verses have never been fulfilled, we need to
ask these questions NOW to see if they find a present application.

1. Has Israel no sons?
2. Has he (Israel) no heir?
3. Why *then* does Milcom inherit Gad, And his people
   dwell in its cities?

The answers to these questions, if asked today, would be as follows;

1. *YES, Israel has sons!* Israel was the name given to Jacob in Genesis 32:28. Jacob had twelve sons and they are referred to as the twelve tribes of Israel. One of the sons was named Gad, (Genesis 30:11). Gad is alluded to in this Jeremiah prophecy. Gad's descendants are part of the modern day regathering of the Jews into Israel. Hitler's genocidal attempt of the Jews, as well as all of the other pogroms to eradicate the Jews throughout history, were unsuccessful. This means that Jacob still has descendants (sons) living today!

2. *YES, Israel has heirs!* Jews are living in Israel as inheritors of the Promised Land given to Abraham! The land was renamed Israel in 1948. It was supposed to have included the ancient tribal territory of Gad as per the Balfour Declaration of 1917. However, the British Empire failed to implement this declaration. This deprived the Jews of obtaining their territorial inheritance of Gad. Gad's territory is situated in Jordan near its capital city of Amman. It is located east of the Jordan River, due north from the Dead Sea. Worsening matters, this territory was snatched away from the Jews and willfully given to the Arabs in 1946. This was accomplished through the "Treaty of London," which was signed between the United Kingdom and Transjordan. This was the same year that Transjordan was renamed Jordan.

3. The third question only applies if the answers to first two questions are YES! If the answers are no, then Jordanians could easily inherit the tribal territory of Gad, because none of Gad's descendants would be alive to stop them. Furthermore, the Jordanians could worship Allah or any false god of their choosing, because Gad's God Jehovah

would be a proven joke! Thus, question number three would be utterly embarrassing for Gad's God Jehovah to have Jeremiah ask. However, the answers to questions one and two are emphatically YES, which means that the Jordanians and their false god, which in the case of today is Allah, are trespassing in the Holy Land!

A practical illustration of the scenario about Jordan's occupation of the tribal territory of Gad is offered below.

Mr. Israel Cohen, *representing God in this story*, is a very wealthy land owner. One of his many Real Estate holdings is a sizable piece of property worth lots of money. The precious real estate is monetarily valuable for two reasons. *First*, it is situated in a prime location. It exists in the most prestigious region of a neighboring nation, *which represents modern day Jordan in this scenario*. *Second*, it is several hundred thousand acres with lots of development potential.

Israel Cohen has a son named Gad, *who represents present day Israel*. Gad is heir to this part of his father's vast empire, which includes this precious piece of property. One day a gang of thugs encroached onto Mr. Cohen's property. Since the estate had been vacant for a long time, the criminals decided to permanently take up residence on the property. They quickly erected homes and moved their wives and young children onto the property.

After a period of time, Mr. Cohen said to his son Gad, *"It's time for you to take ownership of the property that was meant for you as part of your inheritance."* The Son graciously accepted and prepared to possess this invaluable piece of land.

However, when the young man showed up at the property he found the interlopers who were illegally occupying what should have been his property. They had become so numerous that he could not find anyone to prosecute their eviction. So Gad returned to his homeland to enlist his father's support.

Finally, when Mr. Israel Cohen and his legal representatives arrived on the scene they asked the offenders; *"Are you aware that Mr. Israel Cohen is the legal owner of this property? Did you know that he has recently conveyed the ownership of this property over to his heir Mr. Gad Cohen? Do you realize that under the laws of this country you are trespassing, which is a criminal offense?*

The interlopers conceded that the answer was YES to all of the questions, but in the same breath they defiantly declared, *"We don't care what you say! This is our property now!"*

Upon hearing their reply Mr. Israel Cohen declared, *"Had you not been so insolent, I would have extended you some leniency for taking advantage of my uninhabited property. But, because you have refused my son's rightful occupation of this property, your rebellion will cost you greatly. You will receive your just reward, which will be the destruction of your homes, and violent eviction from the property."*

This is the similar scenario that is presently taking place with Jordan. They are nothing more than hoodlums worshipping Allah in the Promised Land that the Lord has given the Jews. They will be evicted and receive a full sentence of divine punishment for their insolent behavior.

Jordan Trembles to the North and Northeast (ISIS)

Jeremiah 49:5 says that the Lord will *"bring fear upon"* Jordan from *"all those who are around."* Presently, Jordan faces trouble on every front. ISIS has its sights on Jordan and is pressing in from the north and northeast from strongholds in Syria and Iraq. This is problematic because ISIS has sympathizers residing inside of Jordan, like they do in Iraq and Syria. Confirming this legitimate concern, the Al Arabia news headline from August 31, 2014 read,

"ISIS' appeal presents Jordan with new test."[42]

The Iraqi and Syrian partisans played a significant role in the expansion of ISIS into those countries. The ISIS supporters in Jordan, like their Iraqi and Syrian counterparts, embrace the same goal of an Islamic State in the Levant (ISIL), which is another acronym that ISIS goes by. The goal of ISIL is to establish their Sunni style of Islamic rule throughout the Levant first, and then extend it throughout the rest of the world.

The concern is that in its bid for more control of the Mideast, ISIL will lockstep with their Jordanian adherents to capture all or parts of Jordan. This approach has already proven to be successful in Iraq and Syria.

Compounding Jordan's internal affairs problems are the hundreds of thousands of Syrian refugees that continue to flood into the country. Presently, there are over 600,000 refugees encamped in Jordan. Many of these exiles are prime candidates for ISIS recruitment.

Jordan Trembles to the East (Iran)

On the eastern front Jordan is unnerved by Iran's attempt to spread its hegemony in its direction. Presently, Iranian troops are deployed into the embattled areas of Iraq and Syria. Moreover, Iran's funding of terrorist organizations like Hezbollah, (to the north) Hamas, (to the west) and the Houthis, (to the south) further aggravates Jordan's situation.

Of equal or greater concern is Iran's burgeoning nuclear program and unhindered development of intercontinental ballistic missiles (ICBM). These ICBM's, which are designed to carry weapons of mass destruction, could fly over Jordanian airspace on route to Israel or America, or even land in Jordan itself.

Jordan Trembles to the West (Israel vs. Hezbollah Conflict)

Hezbollah's growing presence to Jordan's north in the Golan Heights, intensifies the already existing tension between Israel and Syria. On Jordan's western front, Israel is bracing for another possible war with Hezbollah, which could eventuate in over 1500 missiles being launched into Israel daily. A related news headline from Israel National News on April 1, 2015, reads,

"IDF Scenario for Next Hezbollah War: 1,500 Missiles Per Day."[43]

During the 34 day conflict between Israel and Hezbollah in the summer of 2006, Hezbollah launched about 4000 missiles into Israel. This caused many northern Israelis to seek safety in nearby bomb shelters. In anticipation, Israel is fitting some of its bomb shelters with high speed wireless Internet capabilities. Israelis refuged underground, for perhaps weeks at a time, will need to know what's happening to their country.

"Project "Bomb Shelters Online" Underway in Northern Israel" – Israel National News (June 1, 2015)[44]

Once serving as a buffer state between Israel and the broader Muslim dominated Middle East, Jordan is on the verge of becoming more of a liability than an asset to the survival of the Jewish state. This is partially because the Jordanian Armed Forces are no military match for all the firepower mobilizing around it.

The Royal Jordanian Army is mainly in place to preserve the posterity of King Abdullah II and his ruling Hashemite kingdom. In the likely event of an ISIS external aggression against Jordan, and / or subversion from within Jordan, Israel could be drawn into the conflict. Israel has hinted in the past that it would, if Jordan requests, ally with Jordan against ISIS. A news headline from the Jerusalem Post reads,

"Israel, US prepared to help Jordan fight ISIS."[45]

Jordan Trembles to the South (Terror in the Sinai)

Terrorism in the Sinai to Jordan's south complicates matters further because much needed natural gas resources from there are under constant threat. The Ansar Bayt al-Maqdis Sinai based terrorist group, who has pledged allegiance to ISIS, has bombed gas pipelines into Jordan in the recent past. Terrorist groups like this that align with ISIS are another growing concern for Jordan. Like Ansar Bayt al-Maqdis, the Jabhat al-Nusra terrorist organization based in Syria has also joined with ISIS.

"ISIS Affiliate (Ansar Bayt al-Maqdis) Expands in Egypt"
U.S. News and World Report (December 2, 2014)[46]

Jordan Trembles Internally (The Palestinians)

These scenarios above are just a few of the geo-political concerns that prompted Jordan's King Abdullah II to come to Washington in February and December of 2014 and again in February, 2015. These visitations were primarily intended to enlist America's strategic support against the spread of ISIS in the region, and to move the Palestinian – Israeli peace talks forward.

There are an estimated 3.24 million[47] Palestinians living in Jordan, nearly one-half of the country's overall population, many of which are discontent with the current Jordanian leadership. From King Abdullah's perspective, peace between the Palestinians and Israelis could provide some respite to the internal political strife occurring inside of Jordan. These Palestinians want a state of their own or at least more civil liberties within Jordan. King Abdullah's trio of visits to Washington between 2014 - 2015 evidences his fears for what is transpiring within and around Jordan.

With all the geo-political mayhem surrounding him, King Abdullah II is justifiably fretting about his and his country's future. Since the Arab Spring in 2011, he has seen the removal of longstanding leaders and allies in Egypt, Tunisia, Libya, Yemen and recently in Saudi Arabia, with the death of King Abdullah bin Abdul-Aziz. With the passing of these old guards, the Jordanian king finds himself much more reliant on the strange bedfellows of America and Israel for his posterity.

Why Jordan and Why NOW?

Presuming all the above is what drives the fear spoken of in Jeremiah's ancient prediction, the questions are *why Jordan*; and *why NOW?* After all, Jordan maintains a peace treaty with Israel, and is generally pro-western and is regarded by many as the most moderate Arab state in the Middle East.

Some Bible teachers believe that Jordan is a sincere and long lasting friend of Israel's. I have even heard a prophecy expert suggest that Psalm 83 can't be a future prophecy because Jordan is in the Psalm as one of the Arab confederates. He reasoned that Jordan won't betray Israel's trust and join the other Psalm 83 countries to attack Israel. However, Jordan's present friendly relations with Israel appear rosy on the surface but they are thorny underneath. It is important not to overlook the following significant facts;

1. War prophecies concerning Jordan in Jeremiah 49:1-6, Zephaniah 2:8-11, Psalm 83, Ezekiel 25:14, Isaiah 11:14 and elsewhere remain unfulfilled,
2. The wars involving Jordan against Israel in 1948, 1967 and 1973, which did not fulfill all of the prophecies above, demonstrated a clear pattern of hatred toward Israel in modernity,
3. Jordan refuses to acknowledge Israel's right to exist as the Jewish state,
4. Jordan threatened to revoke its 1994 peace agreement with Israel in October of 2014, because Israel threatened Jordan's control over the Temple Mount in Jerusalem,
5. Jordan temporarily withdrew its Ambassador to Israel in November of 2014, also over the Temple Mount matter.
6. About one-half of Jordan's population are Palestinians who are predominately hostile toward Israel.

The answers to *why Jordan* and *why Now* are found in the unfulfilled prophecies of Jeremiah, Zephaniah, Ezekiel, Isaiah and the others listed in #1 above. The element of fear overtaking Jordan is only a small part of the country's foretold future. These prophecies predict that Jordan will also be toppled!

Jeremiah 49:1-2, Zephaniah 2:8-9 and Amos 1:13 point out that Jordan is guilty of enlarging its borders at Israel's expense. Jordan is located within the borders of the "Promised Land" given to the Israelites through Abraham (Genesis 15:18), Isaac (Gen. 26:4) and Jacob (Gen. 28:13). This land spans from the Nile River in Egypt to the Euphrates in Iraq and Syria.

From the biblical perspective, Jordan is trespassing on prime property that was granted by God to Israel. This is land that Israel could use to secure and enlarge its borders. The Lord's prophetic plan, which is ongoing presently, was to regather the Jews from the nations of the world into the re-established nation of Israel as the Jewish state. Throughout most of Jordan's modern history, it has been an obstacle to this sovereign strategy.

Some of the most scathing prophecies in store for Jordan's future deals with the ancient territory of Edom, which is modern day Southern Jordan. According to Amos 1:11, Ezekiel 25:12, 35:5 and elsewhere, Edom has hated Israel with a vengeance. The Bible describes it as a perpetual hatred, which means that it stems from long ago and still exists today. This perpetual enmity against the Jews is represented in the Palestinians, who have Edomite descendants within their ethnicity.

The Palestinian prognosis is very bad because of this hatred of Israel. The two most condemning verses that attest to this are below.

> "I will lay My vengeance on Edom (*Southern Jordan*) by the hand of My people Israel, (*IDF*) that they may do in Edom according to My anger and according to My fury; and they shall know My vengeance," says the Lord GOD."

> — Ezekiel 25:14; *emphasis added*

"The house of Jacob (IDF) shall be a fire, And the
house of Joseph (IDF) a flame; But the house of Esau
(Edomites) *shall be* stubble; They shall kindle them and
devour them, And no survivor shall *remain* of the house
of Esau, (Edomites)" For the LORD has spoken."

— Obadiah 1:18, *emphasis added*

Edom experiences two judgments in the end times. One is
against the Edomite people and the other is against the land of
Edom. Ezekiel 35:9-10 also addresses these two judgments. They
predict that the land of Edom will be perpetually desolate and the
people of Edom will be judged for their hatred of Israel.

Isaiah 34 describes a slaughter in Edom so severe that Southern Jordan will be desolate throughout the 1000 year Messianic
Kingdom period.

"It (Edom) shall not be quenched night or day; Its smoke
shall ascend forever. From generation to generation it shall
lie waste; No one shall pass through it forever and ever."

— Isaiah 34:10; *emphasis added*

I explain these prophecies in greater detail in my book entitled, "*Psalm 83: The Missing Prophecy Revealed, How Israel Becomes
the Next Mideast Superpower.*"

In the prophetic scheme of things, Jordan's peace treaty with
Israel is geo-politically expedient and paper thin. After soundly
losing three conventional wars in 1948, 1967 and 1973 against
Israel, Jordan's former King Hussein found it lucrative economically, geographically, militarily and politically to befriend Israel.
This was not, and is still not, considered to be a popular move by
the majority of the Muslim world, which is mostly pro-Palestinian
and anti-Israel.

Why Jordan and *why NOW?* It's because in order for the Lord to uphold His holy name in Ezekiel 39:7, the Jordanian prophecies have to happen. Jordan can't continue to defiantly ignore Israel's right to exist as the Jewish state, when soon the Lord intends to uphold his holiness through the Jews and Israel. Nor can they possess strategic parts of the Promised Land when Israel needs to utilize it for economic, security and immigration purposes.

If Jordan would only comply with the Lord's compassionate Mideast Peace Plan in Jeremiah 12:14-17, then things could be different for the Arab nation. These Jeremiah verses encourage the Arab states to learn the ways of the one true God of the Bible. If they would, they could live in peace alongside of Israel. But, the one true God of the Bible is JEHOVAH, and not Allah! Jordanians are presently guilty of homesteading the holy land and worshipping a false God. These are the very condemning factors identified in the rhetorical questions of Jeremiah 49:1.

Jordan is beginning to tremble about the uncontrollable chaos that is happening all around its borders. This concern could easily burgeon into the fear and trembling predicted in Jeremiah 49:5. If it is the trembling spoken of, then the toppling of Jordan in Jeremiah 49:2 could happen soon as another *NOW* prophecy.

Psalm 83: The ISIS and Jordan connection

Psalm 83 presents a very problematic prophecy concerning Jordan's future. It identifies Jordan as the "children of Lot," who were Ammon and Moab. Ammon and Moab team up in a ten member Arab confederacy that wants to wipe Israel off of the map and ultimately take possession of the Promised Land. The toppling of Jordan that is predicted in Jeremiah 49:1-5 probably results when Israel wins the Psalm 83 war.

Psalm 83:8 predicts that Jordan will be supported by Assyria, which also participates in the Psalm 83 Arab confederacy. If ISIS continues to expand, they might be a participant in Psalm 83 under the banner of Assyria. On December 26, 2014, I authored an article entitled, "Is ISIS in Psalm 83?"[48] The article pointed out this prophetic possibility. Below are excerpts from that article.

ISIS is the acronym for the Islamic State of Iraq and Syria. "ISIS" is also known as "IS," which simply means the Islamic State and "ISIL," which stands for the Islamic State of Iraq and the Levant. The term ISIL, was adopted by the group after making sweeping territorial gains in Northern Syria and Northern Iraq. The subsequent name changes implied that the organization would seek further regional advances.

The Levant is a term that generally identifies the greater Middle East region, which includes Syria, Jordan, Israel, Lebanon, the Gaza Strip, West Bank, parts of the Sinai, Egypt and Saudi Arabia. Coincidentally, all of these territories appear to be involved in the prophecy of Psalm 83.

There may be a possible correlation in Psalm 83:8 between ISIS, as Assyria, and Jordan. Listed below and explained afterward, are several reasons that this connection might be justified.

- *The Ancient Territory of Assyria*: The swaths of territory now in the possession of ISIS, closely resembles the lands controlled by Assyria at the time that the Psalm was authored.
- *The Dominant Role of Assyria in Psalm 83*: Assyria appears to play a dominant role within the Psalm 83 confederacy. ISIS is presently becoming a dominant actor in the Mideast Theater.
- *The Assyrian-Jordanian Connection*: The Psalm makes a definite connection between Assyria and Jordan, which is possibly another country that ISIS will seek to invade.
- *The True Jordanian Descendants*: The current ruling Hashemite Kingdom of Jordan, has not directly descended from the Ammonites, Moabites and Edomites. These three peoples are listed in Psalm 83 as the true indige-

nous ancestors of the Jordanians today. Therefore, Jordan's current regime may be ousted prior to the fulfillment of Psalm 83.

CAVEAT: *Before explaining the potential prophetic implications of the list above, it is important to note that ISIS could fade off of the world scene as suddenly as it emerged. ISIS could wind up being like the Muslim Brotherhood or the Hamas, which in times past have dominated the news, but now can scarcely command a back page news story. Therefore, it is important to treat the possible ISIS involvement in Psalm 83 as conjecture until proven otherwise.*

EXPLORING THE ISIS and PSALM 83 CONNECTIONS

The Ancient Territory of Assyria

Probably the most interesting possible connection between ISIS of today, and Psalm 83 of yesterday, is the ancient territory of Assyria. When Psalm 83 was penned about 1000 B.C., Assyria mainly encompassed Northern Syria and Northern Iraq. Although the Assyrian Empire expanded significantly a few centuries later when it conquered Damascus in 732 B.C. and the Northern Kingdom of Israel in 722 B.C., at the time that the Psalm was issued Assyria looked much like what ISIS presently possesses.

The Dominant Role of Assyria in Psalm 83

Within the Arab confederacy of Psalm 83, Assyria appears to play a most prominent role. Psalm 83:8 specifically says that Assyria joins with and helps Jordan in the Psalm 83 conflict. Presently, the Jordanian army represents one of the weakest members within the Psalm 83 confederacy. The Jordanian Armed Forces exist in a defensive capacity, and their primary goal is to maintain the supremacy over Jordan of the ruling Hashemite kingdom.

Below is a comparison of the army rankings of the other probable countries involved in Psalm 83.[49] This comparison doesn't take into consideration that Hezbollah in Lebanon has about 150,000 missiles that are not included in Lebanon's ranking. Nor, does it factor in the fighting power of ISIS in Syria's or Iraq's rankings. With the inclusion of these facts, the argument can be made that Jordan's army will desperately need Assyria (perhaps ISIS) as an ally in this concluding Arab-Israeli war.

1. Egypt #13
2. Saudi Arabia #25
3. Syria #26 (not including ISIS)
4. Jordan #67
5. Iraq #68 (not including ISIS)
6. Lebanon #83 (not including Hezbollah)

The Assyrian-Jordanian Connection

The point was made above that Assyria plays a dual role in Psalm 83. They fight against Israel alongside their Arab cohorts, but they also appear to closely align themselves with Jordan in the epic battle. The verse below says that Assyria joins with and helps the children of Lot, which represents Jordan. The children of Lot were Ammon and Moab. Today, Ammon represents Northern Jordan and Moab is associated with Central Jordan.

> *"Assyria also has joined with them; They have helped the children of Lot. Selah"*
>
> — Psalm 83:8

The Hebrew word for "joined" is "*lavah*," and it can be translated as allied, or to stand with. In correlation, the Hebrew word for "helped" is "*zeroa*," and it can mean a strong shoulder of support or armed forces.[50] What Psalm 83 appears to be describing is Assyria becoming a strong ally of Jordan's in the Psalm. They apparently not only align themselves with Jordan, but they somehow fortify Jordanian forces in the fight.

The True Jordanian Descendants

It is important to note that the current ruling regime in Jordan is of the Hashemite kingdom. The Hashemites appear to be descendants of Ishmael, and not from Lot's children, Ammon and Moab. This means that the Hashemites are, at best, distant cousins to the Ammonites and Moabites, and as such, they don't necessarily have any ancestral territorial claims to the modern day country of Jordan. Ishmael is thought to have generally settled in the land which best represents Saudi Arabia today.

Although the Ishmaelites are also listed among the Psalm 83 members, Assyria does not join with and help them according to the prophecy. This might imply that King Abdullah II, the current ruler of Jordan, may be deposed and his ruling Hashemite kingdom dethroned, on or before the fulfillment of Psalm 83. Arab leaders being deposed, assassinated or simply dying off has become fairly commonplace since the inception of the Arab Spring in January of 2011. Gone are Hosni Mubarak of Egypt, Mohamad Morsi of Egypt, Muammar Gaddafi of Libya, Ali Abdullah Saleh of Yemen, Zine El Abidene Ben Ali of Tunisia and King Abdullah Bin Abdul Aziz of Saudi Arabia.

Presently, the true children of Lot appear to be integrated within the Palestinians. The Palestinians are a conglomeration of predominately Arab peoples, but Ammonite and Moabite descendants are among them. Approximately one-half of Jordan's population is comprised of Palestinians and many of them are not supportive of the ruling Hashemite minority. In fact, some of them are pro-ISIS, because as Sunni Muslims, they empathize with the plan of ISIS to establish a Sunni led Islamic Caliphate in the Levant.

If ISIS goes unchecked and continues to burgeon, then it's entirely possible that this terrorist entity will invade Jordan. If they are successful, they could possibly become aligned with the children of Lot as a dominant shoulder of strength in Psalm 83.

Whether or not this will be the case, Jordan's immediate future looks bleak. According to Jeremiah 49:1-5, they will first *tremble*, and second they will be *toppled*. However, Jeremiah 49 has some good news for the Jordanians. This verse foretells that sometime after Jordan gets toppled, some of the Jordanian exiles will acknowledge that Jehovah is God and that Jesus Christ is their Savior.

> *"But afterward I will bring back The captives of the people of Ammon," says the LORD."*

— *Jeremiah 49:6*

14

The Terrorization Of Egypt

The Terrorization of Egypt

Creation of Israel		EZEKIEL 38
	68 YEARS	ISAIAH 19:16-18
1948	2016	20??

These are the days when the Bible is its own best commentary. Imagine Isaiah the prophet, whose ministry[51] spanned between 740-701 B.C., standing on the streets of Cairo during the Arab Spring of 2011, speaking in front of a mainstream news camera declaring:

"The Arab demonstrations have swiftly moved from Tunisia eastward into Egypt! Egyptians are fighting other Egyptians, the military is being pelted with hundreds of Molotov cocktails as brothers are bludgeoning each other, and neighborhoods are riddled with unrest. The streets of Cairo are filled with violence and civil strife! It's a very dangerous situation here in Tahrir Square."

It's seems eerily reminiscent of what the prophet predicted centuries ago.

"The burden against Egypt. Behold, the LORD rides on a swift cloud, And will come into Egypt; … And the heart of Egypt will melt in its midst. "I will set Egyptians

against Egyptians; Everyone will fight against his brother,
And everyone against his neighbor..."

— Isaiah 19:1-2; *emphasis abbreviated*

Is it possible that Isaiah was foretelling of a prophecy intended for modern times? Will more unrest befall the world's most densely populated and powerful Arab state? This chapter will take a close look at the judgment prophecies concerning Egypt in Isaiah 19 in correlation to Psalm 83.

Isaiah alluded to Egypt 36 times in his 66 chapters, but almost half of his prophetic references to Egypt are found in Isaiah 19. Subsequently, Jeremiah and his contemporary Ezekiel inscribed the word Egypt a combined 97 times. Jeremiah and Ezekiel prophesied during the Babylonian era approximately 150 years after Isaiah's time. All told, the word Egypt is mentioned approximately 565 times within the Bible, and many of these usages are pertinent to prophecies that appear to be presently stage – setting.

From Isaiah's time forward, there were at least three devastating judgments identified in Bible prophecy. These three judgments are as follows;

- *PAST Prophecies*– The Babylonian Judgment, described in Jeremiah 42 – 44, Ezekiel 29:18-19, 30:10 and elsewhere,
- *NOW Prophecies*– The Israeli Defense Forces identified in Psalm 83 and Isaiah 19,
- *LAST Prophecies* – The Antichrist during the "Day of the Lord" referenced in - Ezekiel 30:3-4, Daniel 11:42-43, Joel 3:19 and elsewhere.

Among all of Egypt's prophecies, the most important spiritually speaking for Egyptians, is undoubtedly concerning their national conversion. When all is said and done there will be a remnant of Egyptians that survive to reside in the one-thousand year Messianic kingdom. This is great news for the Egyptians because as this chapter points out, events in Egypt seemingly take a severe swift turn for the worse in the near future.

"In that day, (during the millennial reign of Jesus Christ), Israel will be one of three with Egypt and Assyria—a blessing in the midst of the land, whom the LORD of hosts shall bless, saying, "Blessed *is* Egypt *My people*, and Assyria the work of My hands, and Israel My inheritance.""

— Isaiah 19:24-25; *emphasis added*

These verses identify Egyptians as "*My people*." This is not a classification that presently applies to Egypt, because the nation hosts about 80 million Muslims, which constitutes about 95% of its populous. To be called "My people" requires a belief in the true God, *Jehovah*, of the Bible, rather than the false god, *Allah*, of the Koran. Therefore, this is a title that will be bestowed to Egypt in the Messianic kingdom. This means that Egypt will have a national conversion to Christianity sometime prior to the commencement of the millennium. This can be deduced from the realization that only true believers in Christ can enter into that future dispensation.

However, concerning Egypt's existence during the Messianic kingdom era, Ezekiel informs us that the nation of Egypt will be the lowliest of all the kingdoms present upon the earth at that time.

"It shall be *the lowliest of kingdoms*; it shall never again exalt itself above the nations, for I will diminish them so that they will not rule over the nations anymore."

— Ezekiel 29:15; *emphasis added*

It appears safe to say that this specific prophecy has not yet been fulfilled. Clearly, Egypt today is not the lowliest of kingdoms on earth. In fact, Egypt's army, which is ranked 18th among world armies, is the most powerful among the Arab states. The next closest Arab army in the region would be Saudi Arabia located directly eastward across the Red Sea from Egypt, that is ranked 28th. [52] Moreover, there is a famous saying concerning Egypt that is quoted, "As goes Egypt, so goes the Middle East." There are nearly 83 million people living in Egypt and comparatively only about 27 to 28 million in the Arab state of Saudi Arabia.[53]

Egypt's Past Prophecies

The past Babylonian judgment against Egypt occurred in 568 BC when King Nebuchadnezzar marched upon the country in order to replenish his military budget and arsenals. He had endured a tiring, but successful campaign against Tyre, in modern day Lebanon. Ezekiel identifies the king's military motive for us.

> "Son of man, Nebuchadnezzar king of Babylon caused
> his army to labor strenuously against Tyre; every head
> *was* made bald, and every shoulder rubbed raw; yet
> neither he nor his army received wages from Tyre, for
> the labor which they expended on it. Therefore thus says
> the Lord GOD: 'Surely I will give the land of Egypt to
> Nebuchadnezzar king of Babylon; he shall take away her
> wealth, carry off her spoil, and remove her pillage; and
> that will be the wages for his army. I have given him the
> land of Egypt *for* his labor, because they worked for Me,'
> says the Lord GOD."

> — Ezekiel 29:18-20

Jeremiah chapters 42 – 44 brazenly warned the Jews at the time not to flee to Egypt to avoid this impending confrontation with King Nebuchadnezzar. However, many of his people refused to follow his instructions and migrated into Egypt. As a result, scores of them were killed during the Babylonian conquest of Egypt.

"The LORD has said concerning you, O remnant of
Judah, *'Do not go to Egypt!'* Know certainly that I have
admonished you this day."

— Jeremiah 42:19; *emphasis added*

Subsequently, over the centuries Egypt experienced powerful
events such as the Persian, Greek, Roman, and Ottoman Gentile
empires emerging successively. Then in the aftermath of the collapse
of the Ottoman Empire, which had dominated over the region from
1517 – 1917, and the conclusion of World War I in 1918, on February
28, 1922, Egypt regained its national independence.

Egypt's NOW Prophecies

Developments in Egypt since the Arab Spring in 2011 are preparing this Arab state for the fulfillment of prophecies issued in
Isaiah 19:1-18. These ancient predictions could culminate soon in
Egypt's participation in the Arab – Israeli war under the banner of
the "Hagarenes" described in Psalm 83. As such, a study of Isaiah
19:1-18 will be undertaken at this point.

"The tents of Edom and the Ishmaelites; Moab,
and the Hagarenes;"

— Psalm 83:6, ASV

Before exploring Isaiah 19 it is important to recognize that
these Isaiah prophecies might lead into, or somehow be related to,
the Psalm 83 war, but they could also be independent from Psalm
83. Egypt's role in Psalm 83 is the most controversial of the ten
member confederacy in Psalm 83:6-8.

I share my reasons for including Egypt in Psalm 83 in the Appendix called, "Is Egypt in Psalm 83?" If Egypt is in Psalm 83, and
if Isaiah 19:1-18 relates to Psalm 83, Then these Isaiah prophecies
concerning Egypt should be treated as NOW Prophecies.

Isaiah 19:1-18 Commentary

"The burden against Egypt. Behold, the LORD rides on
a swift cloud, And will come into Egypt; The idols of
Egypt will totter at His presence, And the heart
of Egypt will melt in its midst."

— Isaiah 19:1

The very first sentence speaks about a judgment intended against
Egypt. The judgment is from the Lord and it happens quickly like a
swift cloud moves through the windy sky. Before addressing the typological significance of the swift cloud it's important to understand
that the Lord never renders random judgments upon the nations. In
this case, Egypt has done something deserved of divine judgment. The
clue to Egypt's guilt appears to be described in Isaiah 19:16-18, and
is relative to something between Israel and Egypt. Egypt's foul play
toward Israel will be discussed in the commentary of those verses.

The significance of the *swift cloud* that makes the *idols* of Egypt
totter is that when Egypt's judgment occurs, it doesn't appear to
be a long drawn out process, and it adversely affects the spiritual
bedrock of the entire country, which today is predominately Islam.
Cloud cover creates darkness underneath it. Darkness alluding to a
nation's religious condition depicts a country's spiritual blindness.
Egypt's history at the time of the Hebrew exodus saw a similar
scenario of the Lord riding into Egypt on a swift cloud.

"And the Angel of God, who went before the camp of
Israel, moved and went behind them; and the *pillar of
cloud* went from before them and stood behind them. So
it came between the camp of the Egyptians and the camp
of Israel. Thus it was *a cloud* and *darkness to the one, (Egyptians)* and it gave light by night *to the other, (Hebrews)* so
that the one did not come near the other all that night."

— Exodus 14:19-20; *emphasis added*

In addition to this Exodus 14 usage, clouds in relationship to spiritual matters are found in 1 Thessalonians 4:17 describing Christians caught up into the clouds during the Rapture. Also, in Exodus 19:9, the Lord visited Moses via a cloud, and in Exodus 24:15-16, after six days of cloud cover over Mount Sinai, the Lord called out to Moses from the cloud on the seventh day.

These are just a few biblical instances where clouds are used as a typological representation of a deep – seated spiritual matter.

> "I will set Egyptians against Egyptians; Everyone will fight against his brother, And everyone against his neighbor, City against city, kingdom against kingdom."
>
> — Isaiah 19:2

This is another prophetic verse that does not appear to have found fulfillment. Because the idols of Egypt are tottering and the heart of the country is melting in its midst, severe civilian unrest begins to occur. This civil strife quickly burgeons into a civil war, but doesn't stop there. Ultimately kingdoms begin to clash with each other. In this instance "kingdom against kingdom" appears to allude to a regional conflict. Presently there are three predominate kingdoms in the region, the Jewish, Arab, and Persian, and observably they are all mostly at odds with each other.

- Most Arab countries don't recognize Israel's right to exist, and want the Jewish state to give up large portions of land for one more Arab state called Palestine.
- Most Arab countries are genuinely concerned that Iran wants to attain a nuclear weapons program in order to control the balance of power in the Middle East.
- Iran (Persian) is threatening to wipe the Jewish kingdom off of the map.

Isaiah 19:2 predicts a regional conflict in Egypt's future. We see in Isaiah 19:16-18 that this conflict appears to be between the Arab and Jewish kingdoms.

> "The spirit of Egypt will fail in its midst; I will destroy their counsel, And they will consult the idols and the charmers, The mediums and the sorcerers. And the Egyptians I will give Into the hand of a cruel master, And a fierce king will rule over them," Says the Lord, the LORD of hosts."

> — Isaiah 19:3-4

If this prophecy is for our time then these verses imply that when the swift judgment comes, the Egyptians will consult their Muslim clerics and imams to no avail. Their Islamic counsel fails in the midst of the deteriorating matters, which ultimately makes Egypt susceptible to the takeover of a cruel dictator.

Some commentaries suggest that this cruel master was the Assyrian king Esarhaddon, who conquered Egypt in 671 B.C. Another candidate is the Babylonian King Nebuchadnezzar in 568 B.C. The Antichrist is yet another possibility since he is involved in a LAST prophecy against Egypt in Daniel 11:42-43. I think it could even be an Egyptian leader that turns into a ruthless dictator, rather than a foreign national like Esarhaddon, Nebuchadnezzar, or the Antichrist.

> "The waters will fail from the sea, And the river will be wasted and dried up. The rivers will turn foul; The brooks of defense will be emptied and dried up; The reeds and rushes will wither. The papyrus reeds by the River, by the mouth of the River, And everything sown by the River, Will wither, be driven away, and be no more. The fishermen also will mourn; All those will lament who cast hooks into the River, And they will languish who spread nets on the waters. Moreover those

who work in fine flax And those who weave fine fabric
will be ashamed; And its foundations will be broken. All
who make wages *will be* troubled of soul."

— Isaiah 19:6-10

These five verses will be commented upon collectively. At the
time of Egypt's swift calamity, the economy entirely collapses. The
fishing and textile industries that have historically been Egypt's main-
stay will go bankrupt. Tourism could be added into these passages
as well. Although tourism was not a big source of revenue for Egypt
during Isaiah's time, it has been throughout the 20th and 21st centuries.

Isaiah concludes by saying that "All who make wages *will
be* troubled of soul." This statement sums up Egypt's entire economic predicament. Egypt experiences an utter economic collapse.
Egypt's economy is already heading in this direction quite rapidly.
They are reliant upon foreign aid from Saudi Arabia, America, Turkey, and elsewhere now more than ever before. The Arab Spring
may have brought changes politically, but as of yet, it has not improved Egypt economically.

"Surely the princes of Zoan *are* fools; Pharaoh's wise
counselors give foolish counsel. How do you say to
Pharaoh, "I *am* the son of the wise, The son of ancient
kings?" Where *are* they? Where are your wise men? Let
them tell you now, And let them know what the LORD
of hosts has purposed against Egypt. The princes of Zoan
have become fools; The princes of Noph are deceived;
They have also deluded Egypt, *Those who are* the main-
stay of its tribes. The LORD has mingled a perverse
spirit in her midst; And they have caused Egypt to err
in all her work, As a drunken man staggers in his vomit.
Neither will there be *any* work for Egypt, Which the
head or tail, Palm branch or bulrush, may do."

— Isaiah 19:11-15

To understand Isaiah's chastisements in these verses, it is important to note that in the ancient world, Egypt was known for its superior wisdom. Concerning the commentary of these above five verses, The Bible Knowledge Commentary of the Old Testament notates the following in the section that exposits on these verses.

> "Egypt was well known in the ancient world for its wisdom writings and its wise men. But Isaiah warned Egypt not to count on her wise men to save the nation from the coming destruction. The officials of Zoan (vv. 11, 13; cf. Zoan, a city in Egypt's Delta, in Num. 13:22; Ps. 78:12, 43; Isa. 30:4; Ezek. 30:14), the wise counselors of Pharaoh (Isa. 19:11), and the leaders of Memphis (v. 13; cf. Jer. 2:16; 44:1; 46:14, 19; Ezek. 30:13, 16; Hosea 9:6) thought their wisdom might save them from their coming judgment. But their wisdom was foolishness compared with the wisdom of the Lord Almighty who was planning the onslaught. No one in Egypt could do anything to avert the destruction; they were like staggering drunkards before the Lord. Neither the leaders (the head and the palm branch) nor the populace (the tail and the reed; cf. Isa. 9:15) could hold back God's judgment. At one time Zoan was Egypt's capital city (ca. 2050-1800). Memphis, on the Nile about 20 miles north of Cairo, was the first capital of united Egypt (ca. 3200 b.c.) and one of the major cities during much of its long history."

These comments illustrate that at the time the Isaiah 19 prophecy was issued, the pinnacle people and places in Egypt would be affected by this judgment. "The head or tail, Palm branch or bulrush," refers to everyone in Egypt no matter what their station of life was at the time. No Egyptian, whether they are the president of a successful corporation or an ordinary pauper, seems to escape the powerful grasp of Isaiah's burden against Egypt.

> "In that day Egypt will be like women, and will be afraid and fear because of the waving of the hand of the LORD of hosts, which He waves over it. And the land of Judah

will be a terror to Egypt; everyone who makes mention
of it will be afraid in himself, because of the counsel of
the LORD of hosts which He has determined against it."

— Isaiah 19:16-17

Up until these telling verses, we have only been able to ascer-
tain the adverse effects of Isaiah's prophecy, but now we get a clue
to the underlying cause of Egypt's judgment. Isaiah starts by attrib-
uting all the events of Isaiah 19:1-15 to the consequences of Isaiah
19:16-17 by saying, "In that day." In essence, at the time that
Egypt's wisdom fails, religious leaders falter, economy collapses,
and Egypt is ruled by a harsh dictator, the country will be likened
to a fearful woman that has become terrorized by Israel (Judah).

This implies that Egypt has confronted Israel, and in the process provoked a powerful retaliatory response from the Jewish state.
More than likely, this confrontation finds association with Egypt's
military participation in the Psalm 83 war. These verses inform
that Egypt is not terrorized by Babylon, nor by the Antichrist, but
by Judah. This implies that Isaiah 19:1-18 is not addressing the
PAST prophecies with Babylonian conquest, or the LAST prophecies relative to the Antichrist invasion of Daniel 11:42-43, but
rather it seems to speak to the NOW prophecy of Psalm 83, the
final Arab-Israeli war, which appears to be imminent.

Recalling that the Lord doesn't render random judgments,
it makes perfect sense that if Egypt seeks to disavow its current
peace treaty with Israel and confederate with the Psalm 83 Arab
states and terrorist populations in order to destroy the Jewish state,
"that the name Israel be remembered no more," (Psalm 83:4) that
Egypt will be judged! Egypt seeking to curse Israel will provoke
the curse-for-curse in kind clause of Genesis 12:3 to come back
against Egypt.

If the nuclear equipped IDF that is presently ranked #11 among
world armies gets provoked into a war with Egypt, then the odds

are that Egyptians will be terrorized by Judah to the point that they resemble the fearful woman of Isaiah 19:16. Commenting on these two verses, Dr. Arnold Fruchtenbaum writes the following on page 506 of his must read book called the Footsteps of the Messiah;

> *"Never in ancient history has this been true. Only since 1948, and especially since the 6-day war, have the Egyptian forces evidenced the fear portrayed in this passage. There has been fear and dread of Israel ever since. With Egypt having lost 4 wars against Israel with heavy casualties, the fear is deeply rooted. Prophetically, today is still the period of Isaiah 19:16-17."*

"In that day five cities in the land of Egypt will speak the language of Canaan and swear by the LORD of hosts; one will be called the City of Destruction."

— Isaiah 19:18

Again Isaiah prefaces his prophecy by informing us that "In that day," five cities in Egypt will speak the language of Canaan, which is Hebrew. This implies that Israel will annex five cities that are presently under Egyptian sovereignty when the prophecies spelled out in Isaiah 19:1-17 take place. When the IDF defeats the Egyptian army again, then it is possible that they will take more Arab territory. They have a precedent for doing this.

Acquiring land has been a historic pattern for Israel. Joshua did it about 3500 years ago, and King David and his son King Solomon also accomplished this about 3000 years ago. In both instances, the land was annexed in the aftermath of Israeli conquests over the subject Arab territories. Even in modern history this pattern has repeated itself after the IDF victory in the Six Day War in June of 1967. At that time Israel nearly tripled its size by taking over the Gaza, West Bank, Golan Heights, East Jerusalem, and the Sinai Peninsula.

Much of the world considers this "disputed territory," and most of the Arab's call it "occupied territory." However, according to Genesis 15:18 the Bible identifies it as the Promised Land for the exclusive use of the Jewish people. Inside of the Promised Land is all of the land acquired in 1967 and probably much of the land east of the Nile river that is yet to be annexed. It is possible that the five cities Isaiah 19:18 identifies will be located east of the Nile and will be acquired after Egypt's defeat in Psalm 83.

The LAST prophecies concerning Egypt are explained in my book entitled, *"Psalm 83: The Missing Prophecy Revealed, How Israel Becomes the Next Mideast Superpower."* As part of the NOW or LAST Egyptian prophecies, Egypt gets desolated for forty years and the Egyptians are dispersed out of Egypt during those forty years. This is all predicted in Ezekiel 29.

During those forty years, Egypt becomes the lowliest kingdom upon the earth in fulfillment of Ezekiel 29:15. I personally believe and teach that this forty year period results from the LAST prophecy of Egypt, and that it possibly overlaps into the first few decades of the millennium.

Summary

Somewhat similar to the way that Jordan will tremble and be toppled, Egypt will be terrorized and partially toppled. The NOW prophecies of Jordan and Egypt result in Israel expanding territorially. Israel appears to take much of Jordan according to Jeremiah 49 and Zephaniah 2, and at least five cities in Egypt in Isaiah 19:18. Isaiah says one of those cities will be called, "The City of Destruction." This could imply that it was destroyed by Israel, before being taken over by Israel.

Presently, Egypt has a peace treaty with Israel, but according to the NOW and LAST prophecies identified in this chapter, this peace deal is temporary. Someday Egypt, along with Assyria, will possess a permanent peace with Israel according to Isaiah 19:24-25. However, between NOW and then, Egypt will be terrorized according to Isaiah 19:16-18.

15

The Vanishing Of The Christians

Vanishing of the Christians

Creation of Israel		EZEKIEL 38
	68 YEARS	1 Corinthians 15:51-52
1948	2016	20??

O ne night not so long ago, a four year old boy named Colin overheard his daddy and mommy talking about Jesus. They said that Jesus was coming in the clouds to take them away to heaven. He heard his mommy say that Jesus was coming very soon and that in the blink of an eye they would be gone.

It happened to be way beyond Colin's bed time so he kept the matter quietly to himself and crept back into his bed. Colin's cozy little bed was not so comfortable that night; the poor child didn't even sleep a wink. He tossed and turned and cried silently to himself well into the wee hours of the morning.

First thing the next morning, Colin ran in and hugged his mommy and daddy and he wouldn't let go of them. Upon seeing his son crying while embracing them, the father asked, "*What's the matter son?*"

Wiping back his tears, young Colin replied, "*What about me and my baby sister, who will take care of us when Jesus steals you away from us?*"

Realizing that his little preschooler must have listened in on his late night conversation with his wife, the dad picked him up and hugged him tightly and said, *"Colin, Jesus is coming for all of us. Jesus is not stealing us away from you and sissy, He's taking us all up to heaven with Him. Because Daddy and Mommy believe in Jesus, we all get to go."*

Was the father right? Is that the correct answer to what takes place when Jesus returns for His Church in the Rapture event? Does it happen that quickly and do the children get raptured along with their parents?

The Rapture is an incredible supernatural event. It involves the instantaneous disappearances, without any warnings, of millions of true believing Christians throughout the world. It is the special occasion when Christ, as the Bridegroom, comes to fetch His bride the Christian Church.

The event is so well documented in the Bible, that when the epic episode takes place, there can be little doubt about what occurred. However, the valid questions are, will it actually happen, and if so, when will it happen?

The timing of when the Rapture occurs is the subject of much controversy. Some believe it will happen before the "Tribulation Period," while others think it will happen during or at the end of this period. The tribulation period covers the last seven years on this present earth's prophetic timeline. This is when the Lord pours His wrath out upon a Christ rejecting sinful humanity. After this period of wrath, the earth will be restored for the millennial reign of Christ. Rather than address the competing views about the timing of the Rapture, this chapter will explain why I believe it is an imminent Pre-Tribulation event.

The most descriptive verses about the Rapture are found in 1 Corinthians 15:51-53 and 1 Thessalonians 4:15-18, which are quoted below. A close examination of these passages makes it difficult to interpret them in any other way but literally. Since the Bible is the infallible Word of God, and is correct in every detail, the Rapture will happen!

> For this we say to you by the word of the Lord, that we [*believers*] who are alive *and* remain until the coming of the Lord will by no means precede those [*deceased believers*] who are asleep. For the Lord [*Jesus Christ*] Himself will descend from heaven with a shout, with the voice of an archangel, and with the trumpet of God. And the dead in Christ will rise first. Then we who are alive *and* remain shall be caught up together with them in the *clouds* to meet the Lord in the air. And thus we shall always be with the Lord. Therefore comfort one another with these words.
>
> — 1 Thessalonians 4:15-18; *emphasis added*

These verses describe an incredible event, the likes of which have never been witnessed anywhere, or at any time upon the earth. When this miraculous episode occurs precisely as predicted, then a multitude of living people are going to disappear from the face of the earth. These individuals are going to defy the laws of gravity and ascend upward in the air into the clouds.

Concerning the expediency of the event, 1 Corinthians says,

> "Behold, I tell you a mystery: We shall not all sleep, but we shall all be changed—in a moment, *in the twinkling of an eye*, at the last trumpet. For the trumpet will sound, and the dead will be raised incorruptible, and we shall be changed."
>
> — 1 Corinthians 15:51-52; *emphasis added*

These verses inform that in the span of a nanosecond, "*in the twinkling of an eye*," the vanishings take place. When the apostle Paul wrote these two verses about 2000 years ago, the blinking of an eye was the fastest known measurement of time. Paul predicts that, faster than a speeding bullet or the speed of light, scores of people will disappear from sight.

Who goes, does it include men, women and children? Does everyone depart, or only a select group? According to the father in our story above, even the children get to go, but what or who determines this? (The question about the children is addressed later in this chapter).

The key words in the 1 Thessalonian verses above are, "*in Christ.*" It says, "*The dead in Christ will rise first. Then we who are alive and remain shall be caught up together with them.*" The "*we*" referred to are the people alive at the time that are likewise, "*in Christ.*" Christians are the ones that get caught up into heaven. Not Muslims, Hindus, Buddhists or any other non-Christians. Only those that are "*in Christ*" receive a ticket of admission into heaven through this event. To be in Christ is more than believing Christ existed, it means to be a true believer in Christ as your Savior. Only Christ and you know if you are presently, "*in Christ.*"

About 2000 years ago, Jesus Christ came to the earth, died for mankind's sins, was buried for three days in a grave, resurrected from that grave and then ascended to heaven to be with God, the Heavenly Father. Since that time many Christians living in the generations that followed have longed for the blessed hope of His glorious return to Rapture them.

> "For the grace of God that brings salvation has appeared
> to all men, teaching us that, denying ungodliness and
> worldly lusts, we should live soberly, righteously, and
> godly in the present age, looking for the blessed hope
> and glorious appearing of our great God and Savior Jesus
> Christ, who gave Himself for us, that He might redeem
> us from every lawless deed and purify for Himself *His*
> own special people, zealous for good works."
>
> — Titus 2:11-14

The blessed hope of Christ's glorious appearing hasn't happened yet, but could it happen NOW? This chapter will explain why NOW is a distinct possibility, but meanwhile, what has Christ been doing in heaven up until NOW?

Upon His departure from earth, Jesus began preparing habitations in heaven for His faithful followers. He is planning to locate each believer into their own heavenly dwelling place.

> "Let not your heart be troubled; you believe in God, believe also in Me. In My Father's house are many mansions; if *it were* not *so,* I would have told you. I go to prepare a place for you. And if I go and prepare a place for you, I will come again and receive you to Myself; that where I am, *there* you may be also. And where I go you know, and the way you know." Thomas said to Him, "Lord, we do not know where You are going, and how can we know the way?" Jesus said to him, "I am the way, the truth, and the life. No one comes to the Father except through Me.
>
> — John 14:1-6

Jesus says in these verses that He is the only way to get to the Heavenly Father. This again emphasizes that the only way to enter into heaven is to be, "*in Christ.*"

The intent of this chapter's commentary is not to legitimize a literal Rapture event. There are a plethora of good articles and books written on the subject, which have already accomplished this. Recommended websites offering scholarship in this area are duly footnoted here.[54] Moreover, the 1 Thessalonians and 1 Corinthians passages cited above clearly declare that there will be an instantaneous departure of Christians into the clouds to be with Christ forever.

Some argue that the word Rapture is not identified in the Bible. Below are a couple of quotes that address this concern.

"A frivolous argument against the Rapture is that the word cannot even be found in the Bible. If that were true, it would be irrelevant for the names of several biblical concepts are not found in the bible, such as Trinity, Shekinah and the word Bible!... But the fact of the matter is that the word, Rapture, can be found in the Bible. It appears in the Latin Bible in 1 Thessalonians 4:17, where English language Bibles refer to believers being "caught up" to meet Jesus in the sky when He returns for His Church." (Dr. David Reagan).[55]

"Rapture is an English word derived from the Latin word raeptius, taken from the Latin Vulgate translation, which in turn is a translation of the Greek word harpazo. Harpazo is found 13 times in the New Testament. Harpazo means to seize, catch away, caught up or taken away by force. The clearest passage describing the Rapture is found in 1 Thessalonians 4. In this chapter the Apostle Paul describes the "catching away" of the believers to meet the Lord in the Air." (Jim Tetlow) [56]

Christians Escape the Wrath of God

There are several scriptures that teach believers are not going to experience the wrath of God that occurs during the seven year tribulation period.

"But God demonstrates His own love toward us, in that while we were still sinners, Christ died for us. Much more then, having now been justified by His blood, *we shall be saved from wrath* through Him."

— Romans 5:8-9; *emphasis added*

"And to wait for His Son from heaven, whom He raised from the dead, *even* Jesus *who delivers us from the wrath to come.*"

— 1 Thessalonians 1:10; *emphasis added*

"For those who sleep, sleep at night, and those who get
drunk are drunk at night. But let us who are of the day
be sober, putting on the breastplate of faith and love, and
as a helmet the hope of salvation. *For God did not appoint
us to wrath*, but to obtain salvation through our Lord
Jesus Christ, who died for us, that *whether we wake or
sleep, we should live together with Him*"

— 1 Thessalonians 5:7-10; *emphasis added*

Revelation calls it an hour of trial that comes upon the entire
world, which believers are kept from.

"Because you have kept My command to persevere,
I also will keep you from the hour of trial which shall
come upon the whole world, to test those who dwell on
the earth. Behold, I am coming [*Rapture*] quickly! [*In
the twinkling of an eye*] Hold fast what you have, that
no one may take your crown."

— Revelation 3:10-11; *emphasis added*

These passages above teach that believers are *saved, delivered,* and
kept from the wrath of God, but how and when? The Rapture is the
logical explanation for how. 1 Thessalonians 1:10 specifies that Jesus
personally "*delivers us from the wrath to come.*" 1 Thessalonians 5:10 instructs that "*whether we wake or sleep, we should live together with Him.*"

These passages closely parallel the events described above in 1
Thessalonians 4:17-18 that state "*And the dead* (asleep) *in Christ
will rise first. Then we who are alive and remain* (awake) *shall be
caught up together with them in the clouds to meet the Lord* (Jesus) *in
the air. And thus we shall always be with the Lord. Therefore comfort
one another with these words.*"

Believers are to comfort one another with this unique understanding. This is because Christians *escape*, rather than *endure*, the

wrath of God. There are six main reasons below, which argue that believers escape the wrath poured out during the Tribulation period.

The Rapture is a Message of Hope and Comfort

- *First*, the fact believers are instructed to comfort one another by reminding each other about the Rapture implies they won't endure the upheavals of the trib-period. How can one be comforted when they are concerned about experiencing the wrath of God? Therefore the comfort comes when believers remind each other that an escape route exists. This has nothing to do with escaping our earthly responsibilities. In fact, it encourages believers to redeem the time that they have on earth. Imagine if you lived each day as though it were your last, how effectively you would make use of your short time remaining. *Parakaleo*, the Greek word used for comfort, can be translated to mean encourage. In essence, the apostle Paul exhorts believers to encourage one another with reminders of the Rapture.

Nowhere on Earth to Hide from God's Wrath

- *Second*, the tribulation judgments are worldwide, leaving believers no safe-haven from wrath anywhere on earth. Some teach that the Church will be hidden somewhere within the earth from the wrath of God. Revelation 6 argues against this possibility. It presents a vivid description of the entire world as a danger-zone.

"I looked when He opened the sixth seal, and behold, there was a great earthquake; and *the sun* became black as sackcloth of hair, and *the moon* became like blood. And *the stars* of heaven fell to the earth, as a fig tree drops its late figs when it is shaken by a mighty wind. Then *the sky* receded as a scroll when it is rolled up, and *every moun-*

tain and island was moved out of its place. And the kings
of the earth, the great men, the rich men, the command-
ers, the mighty men, every slave and every free man, hid
themselves in the caves and in the rocks of the mountains, and said to the mountains and rocks, "Fall on us
and hide us from the face of Him who sits on the throne
and from the wrath of the Lamb! *For the great day of His
wrath has come, and who is able to stand?*""

— Revelation 6:12-17; *emphasis added*

The *sun, moon, sky, stars, mountains,* and *islands* are all dis-
turbed. These environmental disorders evidence the wrath of God
has come. The text clearly states that everyone from king, slave,
and free man are at a loss to find suitable refuge from the catastrophes of the "*great day of His wrath.*" It does not state everyone,
except the Christians. Unless Christians are somehow herded into
a specially designated corner of the earth beforehand, which goes
against what the text clearly states, they will not be *saved, delivered,
kept,* nor *comforted* from the perilous planetary events.

There were Christians that died on September 11, 2001, when
the twin towers toppled, and there are Christians being persecuted
today in the Middle East and other repressed parts of the world.
But, there doesn't appear to be Christians on earth hiding out in
caves alongside all the unbelievers in Revelation 6:12-17, witnessing God's wrath descend upon mankind.

It is important to note that many left behind unbelievers will become believers during the tribulation period when the wrath of God
is poured out. But, believers up to the point of the Rapture escape this
wrath. The Church, which is analogous with the Bride of Christ,[57] is
fetched by Christ, the Bridegroom, before the wrath begins.

The promise to escape the wrath of God is unique to believer's
that get Raptured. Those who accept Christ after the Rapture are
instructed to be patient even to the pain of death for their rewards

are in heaven. Some of these last day's post-rapture believers exist in a period the book of Revelation identifies as "*the patience of the saints.*"

"If anyone has an ear, let him hear. He who leads into captivity shall go into captivity; he who kills with the sword must be killed with the sword. Here is *the patience* and the faith *of the saints.*"

— Revelation 13:9-10; *emphasis added*

"Here is *the patience of the saints*; here *are* those who keep the commandments of God and the faith of Jesus. Then I heard a voice from heaven saying to me, "Write: 'Blessed *are* the dead who die in the Lord from now on.'" "Yes," says the Spirit, "that they may rest from their labors, and their works follow them.""

— Revelation 14:12-13; *emphasis added*

The Old Testament Allusions to the Rapture

- *Third,* some of the strongest arguments in favor of a Pre-Tribulation Rapture are the models or types that are found in the Old Testament. Though the Rapture was hidden in part from Old Testament believers, the types found throughout the Old Testament foreshadow a future Rapture when God removes His people prior to pouring out His wrath on a Christ-rejecting world. The appendix entitled, "Old Testament Allusions to the Rapture," provides several Old Testament examples of this.

The Church is in Heaven During the Tribulation Period

- *Fourth,* the Church is residing in heaven before the tribulation period commences. This conclusion is supported by understanding the chronological ordering of chapters two through six in the book of Revelation. Revelation 2 and

3 describe the Church on earth while Revelation 4 and 5 pictures the Church residing in heaven. Revelation 6 introduces the earthly events that occur after the Christian Church has been removed from the earth via the Rapture. The prophecies in Revelation 6 segue into the tribulation period. The details of this ordering are explained below.

Revelation 2 and 3 contain the seven letters to the seven Churches. These letters had multiple applications at the time of their issuance. First, they provided important individualized information for the seven specific Churches that they were addressed to. Second, these letters detailed the distinguishing characteristics that would exist at any given time within various Churches throughout the Church age. Third, they outlined the prophetic future of the Church age. In essence, these two chapters portrayed the Church during its existence on earth during the Church age from its inception until its completion.

After the Church age is completed, meaning once it is removed from the earth, Revelation 4 begins with the Greek words *"meta tauta,"* which means *"after these thing,"* and pictures the Church being raptured into heaven. In other words, after these things pertaining to the Church on earth, it is caught up to heaven in Revelation 4 and 5.

> "After these things (*meta tauta*) I looked, and behold, a door standing open in heaven. And the first voice which I heard was like a trumpet speaking with me, saying, "Come up here, [*representing the rapture*] and I will show you things which must take place after this."
>
> — Revelation 4:1; *emphasis added*

It is commonly taught that the twenty-four elders, who are identified several times in Revelation 4 and 5, represent the Church in heaven. Revelation 5:9 informs that these elders are redeemed by the blood of Christ. Only true believers are qualified to make such a salvation claim. Moreover, these redeemed are "*out of every tribe and tongue and people and nation.*" This is an acknowledgement that the twenty-four elders represent the believers saved throughout the world during the Church age.

Sometime after the Church gets caught up into heaven, the events described in Revelation 5 commence. One very significant event that the twenty-four elders witness is the opening of the heavenly scroll by Jesus Christ. This scroll contains the seven seal judgments. The first seal judgment, which is described in Revelation 6:1-2, introduces the Antichrist upon the earth. According to Daniel 9:27, the Antichrist confirms a covenant with Israel for seven years. This is commonly taught to be the starting point of the seven years of the tribulation period.

Therefore, it can be concluded that only when the Church resides in heaven, can it watch Christ open the scroll that contains the seven seal judgments. Until these seal judgments are opened, the Antichrist can't emerge upon the world scene and confirm the seven year covenant with Israel. As long as the covenant can't be confirmed, the tribulation period can't commence. Simply stated, the tribulation period won't begin until sometime after the Christian Church has been raptured into heaven.

The Bride of Christ and the Jewish Wedding Models

- *Fifth*, the Bridegroom (Christ) and Bride (Christian Church) analogy given several times in the New Testament, also infers believers *escape* the wrath. It is doubtful that Christ would come for a bride that has been battered, bruised, and tarnished from seven years of tribulation. Contrarily, it makes more sense that Jesus would return to rapture His believers before they are ravished by those judgments that are specifically intended for unbelievers.

The bride's worthiness is based solely upon her genuine faith in the Bridegroom, and not courageous works performed amidst

the backdrop of tribulation judgments. Believers have nothing further to prove. They are not obligated to undergo the fiery trials
taking place in the trib-period.

> "For by grace you (*believers*) have been saved through
> faith, and that not of yourselves; *it is* the gift of God, *not
> of works*, lest anyone should boast."

— Ephesians 2:8-9; *emphasis added*

Many Christian expositors compare the Bridegroom example to the traditional Jewish wedding model. What could be
more appropriate, considering Christ was a Jew? The following
brief outline of the process was partially taken from notes provided within a related Chuck Missler article called "*The Wedding
Model.*"[58]

a. *Betrothal* – The groom negotiated a fair price (*mohair*) for
    his bride. In the case of believers, the price was paid by
    Jesus Christ's precious sacrificial blood of upon the cross
    for the sins of believers.

b. *Separation* – The engagement period was actually a time
    of separation usually lasting about 12 months. While the
    bride-to-be stayed home, the groom returned to his fa-
    ther's house to make preparations for their future lives to-
    gether. This gave the bride time to prepare her trousseau,
    and the groom to construct a place for the two of them to
    live happily ever after. Presently, Christ and the bride are
    separated. He is in heaven while she is on earth prepar-
    ing her wedding garments, which according to Revelation
    19:8 are her righteous acts.

c. *Preparation* – The groom utilized the separation period to
    return to his father's house to construct the couple's new
    home on the premises. John 14:1-4, identified above,
    points out that is a function Christ is presently perform-

ing in heaven. Believers can expect to inhabit spectacular heavenly abodes because several scriptures point out that Christ is no novice when it comes to carpentry.

"Is this [*Jesus*] not the carpenter, the Son of Mary?"

— Mark 6:3a

This question was asked by Jesus' local countrymen who were astounded by His teaching in the neighborhood synagogue. They had identified him as a carpenter in the past, rather than the prophet He had become.

"He [*Jesus*] is the image of the invisible God, the firstborn
over all creation. For by Him all things were created that
are in heaven and that are on earth, visible and invisible,
whether thrones or dominions or principalities or powers.
All things were created through Him and for Him. And
He is before all things, and in Him all things consist."

— Colossians 1:15-17

The major premise that can be drawn from these Colossians passages is that Jesus can create anything, including thousands of stars, species, varieties of vegetation, and much more. Thus, the minor premise is that He can construct magnificent mansions for his faithful followers.

With this verse in mind, take a moment and imagine the most spectacular manor that you have ever set eyes upon. The dream home that you believed was only achievable in a fairy tale. Then, consider what the apostle Paul wrote in 1 Corinthians 2:9,

*"Eye has not seen, nor ear heard, Nor have entered into
the heart of man the things which God has prepared
for those who love Him."*

Is it conceivable to believe that the "Divine Carpenter," Jesus Christ, will spare any expense when it comes to constructing His bride's happy home? Revelation 21:21 says that the street in the city of "New Jerusalem" will be paved with gold, so it's unimaginable to think that Christ is building Hooverville cardboard shanties.

Some translations of John 14:2 say, "In My Father's house there are many dwellings or rooms, which leads some commentators to wonder if these are actually marvelous mansions. It's worth mentioning that the Greek word used for "*many*" in this verse can also be translated as, *large, larger, very large,* and even *high price.* [59] Maybe when Christ escorts His bride into her heavenly estate, she will say something like, "*In heaven my Bridegroom has prepared many mansions. These are prime properties that are very large.*"

Regardless of their size and quality of construction, I believe it's safe to suggest that presently in heaven,

- The finishing nails are being hammered into the bride's cabinets,
- Her mailbox is firmly planted in the ground and individually addressed,
- The welcome mat has her name inscribed upon it and is laid at the doorstep,
- The believer's furniture has been fixed in place,
- The wedding gown is tailor made to the bride's new resurrected body size,
- Christ is ready to carry His bride over the threshold of her new castle.

d. *Fetching* – At the appropriate time after the construction was completed, the groom came to fetch his bride. Although the bride knew the time would come, she didn't necessarily know precisely when. This is the case with believers today; they know Christ is coming but don't know the day or hour. Also, the groom's arrival was usually accompanied by the best man and several friends. When the party arrived to fetch the bride there was often a shout from the friends to announce the groom had arrived. 1 Thessalonians 4:16 declares there will be a shout announcing Christ's return from His friend the archangel.

e.   *Consummation* – Once fetched, the two returned to the groom's fathers house where they were secluded in a bridal chamber (*huppah*). While inside the chamber they consummated their marriage by entering into physical union for the first time. They remained secluded in the chamber for seven days while the wedding guests enjoyed the wedding feast at the groom's father's house. This will be the similar case with Christ and his believers. Together they will be secluded somewhere in heaven consummating their union, while the seven-years of tribulation take place on earth. The seven-days seem to represent these seven years of tribulation.

f.   *Celebration* - After the seven days had elapsed, the groom brought his bride out of the chamber to greet the wedding guests and partake of the celebration. This will be the case after the trib-period, Christ will reign in His messianic kingdom and his bride will co-reign faithfully by His side.

This Jewish wedding model suggests that believers escape the seven years of tribulation by being safely secluded somewhere in heaven. The question is; do you have your name on one of those doormats? Have you said "I Do" to the wedding proposal of Jesus Christ? It is a matter of receiving Christ as your Lord and Savior. Romans 10:9 states that this is a confession with the mouth of the Lordship of Jesus Christ that is coupled with a heartfelt believe that He was resurrected.

Believers Have a Way of Escape

- *Sixth*, believers are promised by Christ to escape the trib-period.

"But take heed to yourselves, [*bride / believers*] lest your
hearts be weighed down with carousing, drunkenness,
and cares of this life, and that Day come on you unex-
pectedly. For it will come as a snare on all those who
dwell on the face of the whole earth. Watch therefore,
and pray always that you may be counted worthy to
escape all these things that will come to pass, and to stand
before the Son of Man."

— Luke 21:34-36; *emphasis added*

Christ warns His bride to be sober, watchful, and prayerful while
she prepares her trousseau (*righteous acts*). The promise is that she will
be worthy to *escape all these things that will come to pass*, alluding to the
wrath that is to come. She is not being invited to *endure all these things*,
nor is she being informed that she will *escape* only some of *these treacherous things*. No, none of the above, Christ's bride gets a honeymoon suite
specially prepared in heaven, where she goes to escape the wrath of God.

With all that has been written above, I would be remiss not
to remind that the way to say "*I Do*" to such a glorious wedding
proposal is given in Romans 10. The apostle Paul writes;

"That if you confess with your mouth the Lord Jesus and
believe in your heart that God has raised Him from the
dead, you will be saved. For with the heart one believes
unto righteousness, and with the mouth confession is
made unto salvation. For the Scripture says, *"Whoever
believes on Him will not be put to shame."* For there is no
distinction between Jew and Greek, for the same Lord
over all is rich to all who call upon Him. For *"whoever
calls on the name of the Lord shall be saved."*

— Romans 10:9-13

The bride of Christ realizes that it's a matter of saying her "*I
do*" wedding vows; "*I do, confess my faith in Lord Jesus, and I do*

believe in my heart that God raised Him from the dead." Dear reader, if you haven't said your "*I do*" wedding vows as of yet, then you run the risk of *enduring,* rather than *escaping,* the wrath of God by missing out on Christ's return to fetch His bride. Time is of the essence since these are the last days and the Rapture could occur at any moment. You can claim your passport to heaven by receiving Christ in the simple manner presented in the chapter entitled, "*Preparing Spiritually for the NOW Prophecies.*"

Dreaming about the Rapture

The night before authoring this chapter I was praying for a communication from the Lord about it. I was seeking something useful that I could sink my teeth into besides the Rapture insights that other authors have previously covered. I petitioned as follows,

> "*Lord, please give me something, a spiritual epiphany, or an overlooked Scripture, or even a dream or vision that has something to do with the Rapture.*"

Instantly in the prayer, I was reminded that I had already received a relevant dream about the Rapture. It was on a very restful night in December of 2012, when I was caught up into the clouds while sleeping. I remember the dream vividly because it happened during a weeknight between two back to back Sunday sermons that I delivered that December at Calvary Chapel Beachside Church in Huntington Beach, CA.

The second sermon was going to cover the Rapture, so at the time, I marveled to myself about the timeliness of the dream. I shared the dream with the congregation that following Sunday, which got them very excited. Their enthusiasm was driven by the fact that they attend a Church that, like me, believes in a Pre-Trib Rapture.

While being enraptured in the dream-state, I began to levitate effortlessly and uncontrollably upward. "*Oh no, what about the roof? This isn't good,"* was my first thought. That concern lasted about a split second because before I knew it, I was hovering over the roof on the outside and still ascending.

While floating continually upward, I had a second realization, which was, *"I'm being Raptured, oh my God, I'm being Raptured!"* Then a third thought dawned upon me, which was to gaze around to see my immediate surroundings. What I witnessed was startling! I saw others also ascending. They, like me, were each headed into their own designated cloud.

You might be thinking, "why would that astonish the author? After all, it's the Rapture and all of those true believers *"in Christ"* get caught up into the clouds."

What astounded me was my fourth recognition, which was that the crowds drifting upward were few and far between and the cloud cover was extremely sparse. My fifth and final thought before the dream ended was, *"I guess that's what Jesus meant when He spoke about the narrow road that leads to salvation."*

> "Enter by the narrow gate; (Jesus Christ) for wide *is* the gate and broad *is* the way that leads to destruction, and there are many who go in by it. Because narrow *is* the gate and difficult *is* the way which leads to life, and there are few who find it."

> — Matthew 7:13-14, quoting Jesus Christ

CAVEAT: This personal experience was shared because of its potential relevance to this chapter. Please don't base your conclusions about the validity or the timing of the Rapture upon this dream. This dream and the one shared in chapter one, may or may not be significant. I personally believe that they are, but I'm neither asking you to agree or disagree with my assessments. However, considering the fact that in the past couple of decades, tens of thousands of Muslims in the Middle East have been converting to Christianity because of personal dreams and visions, I believed that my two dreams deserved at least an honorable mention in this book.

Jesus says the gateway to salvation is narrow, but is it wide enough to include young Colin and his baby sister that were mentioned at the beginning of this chapter? They were both too young to make a knowledgeable choice to receive Christ. However, Colin's father assured his son that he and his sissy would be Raptured with his believing parents.

This is a sensitive subject, one that concerns many Christian parents or expectant parents today. What happens to the young children, toddlers, babies and the unborns in the wombs, when the Rapture occurs?

Some, like Bible prophecy author Terry James, believe that all of the above will be Raptured. Terry James is also the co-founder of Rapture Ready.com, which is one of the most visited Rapture websites in the world. James goes so far as to suggest that even unborn children in the wombs of Muslim mothers might be taken up into the clouds in the Rapture. Terry shared this opinion with me a few years ago in a radio interview.

Others point out that the Bible is unclear on this subject and cite that during the flood of Noah, the destruction of Sodom and Gomorrah and other historical instances that small children perished alongside their parents. Most Bible scholars agree that the Scriptures do not give a definitive answer from the clear text as to whether or not children, under the age of accountability, will be included in the rapture.

The Age of Accountability

The age of accountability is that critical point in one's life when they are solely responsible to make a personal decision to receive Christ as their Lord and Savior. Once they achieve that age, they can no longer rely on the faith of a parent or on their own youthful innocence as a protective covering over their inherent sin nature. Once they reach that illusive age, they must atone for their own sins by accepting the ultimate sacrifice for all sins, which is the blood of Jesus Christ that was shed upon the cross.

Some disagree whether or not a parent's faith or childhood innocence actually exists. It is not my intent to debate these topics in this short section. More can be learned about childhood sin coverings and whether children automatically go to heaven when they die in these verses, 1 Corinthians 7:14, 2 Samuel 12:20-23, Matthew 19:13-15 and Mark 10:13-16.

The Bible speaks about an age of accountability in at least one place, and that's Isaiah 65:20. Unfortunately, this verse doesn't help us concerning childhood eligibility in the Rapture scenario. This verse deals with the age of accountability in the millennium, which comes into existence after the tribulation period concludes. According to Isaiah a person in the millennium will have up to one hundred years to receive Christ.

"No more shall an infant from there *live but a few* days,
Nor an old man who has not fulfilled his days; For the
child shall die one hundred years old, But the sinner *being* one hundred years old shall be accursed."

— Isaiah 65:20

So what is the answer to the question about children being Raptured? If children aren't saved by a covering faith of a believing parent or childhood innocence, then who takes care of them if they are left behind after the Rapture? What if the child is still in the womb when the Christian mother gets raptured? Does the baby miscarry or somehow survive the ordeal, only to suffer through seven hellish years of tribulation? What if Terry James is correct and a baby of a Muslim mother gets supernaturally extracted from her womb? How will the Muslim mother respond?

So, the question for you, the reader, becomes this. We, as believers, are instructed in Titus 2:13 to look "for that blessed hope, and the glorious appearing of the great God and our savior, Jesus Christ." If Colin was not going to heaven in the rapture with his believing parents, and was going to be left behind to face the greatest tribulation the world has or will ever know, on his own with no parent to protect or guide him in the ways of the Lord, how could any believing parent look forward to this event? The rapture, instead of an event to be eagerly anticipated and looked forward to, would become an event of dread and fore bearing for them, knowing what their loved ones will be facing. So what do you believe the answer is?

My personal view is that Christian parents should comfort one another about the return of Christ in the Rapture, just as they are instructed to do in 1 Thessalonians 4:18. They should do this with the confidence that their young children will be taken up with them into heaven in the Rapture. However, to be on the safe side, remember that the Bible is clear about teaching the young child the ways of the Lord early on. Therefore, get busy from day one of your child's life by loving, praying and teaching that child about Jesus Christ. Even when they are in the womb, sing to them, *"Jesus loves me this I know, for the Bible tells me so."*

A few Scriptures concerning child rearing are Deuteronomy 11:19, Proverbs 22:6, 15 and 13:24, Ephesians 6:4, and Colossians 3:21.

Summary

The timeline image at the beginning of this chapter makes it appear as though the Rapture will happen before Ezekiel 38. For reasons that were shared earlier in this book, I personally believe that it might. However, the Rapture could occur before, during or after Ezekiel 38. Only the Lord knows the precise timing of the Rapture.

Although the timing is unknown, the Bible is very clear that the Lord Jesus Christ is coming to fetch His bride, the Christian Church. When He does, it will happen so suddenly that the bride will be swept off of her feet. Not even a single second will come between their eternal embrace. Together the two of them will ride off into the heavenly sunset and live happily ever after.

Some of those left behind on the earth will recognize that what took place was the Rapture, however many will not. Satan will provide an alternative explanation in order to deceive those that are still stranded upon the earth.

I personally suspect the devilish lie that will be perpetrated in the aftermath of the Rapture will have something to do with the UFO or extra-terrestrial scenarios. I provide a description of how this deceptive situation could happen in my book called, "*Revelation Road, Hope Beyond the Horizon*." The biggest turning point in human history, outside of the crucifixion of Christ upon the cross, will be when mankind recognizes that they are not alone in this universe.

Bible believers already realize this fact because their holy book acknowledges that good and bad angels exist. However, humanity at large doesn't understand the inner workings within the angelic realm. Satan realizes that this prevailing ignorant mentality within humankind exists and he will easily exploit this biblical illiteracy. Dear reader, don't you be caught off guard by Satan's deception, whatever it is, not now and especially not then after the Rapture!

Whatever the alternative explanations to the Rapture are, everyone living before the event has the opportunity to take part in the event. No one now has to stick around to witness what Satan has concocted to occur after the miraculous Rapture. All they have to do is say "*I do*" to the wedding invitation of Jesus Christ, the Bridegroom.

So as an ordained minister let me ask you dear reader, "Do you solemnly swear to take Jesus Christ as your lawfully wedded Husband, to have and to hold forevermore?" If the answer is yes, then live each day as though tomorrow will be the day of your wedding. If you have ever been married, you know the feeling of the night before the wonderful wedding. Live and breathe in that anticipation and comfort one another with these words, because Jesus is coming back for His bride NOW!

16

Preparing Mentally And Physically For The NOW Prophecies

This chapter is designed to prepare the reader mentally and physically for the local and global impacts of the NOW Prophecies. The next chapter prepares you for these events spiritually. The time to get ready for the fulfillment of an epic event is before it happens. If the weather forecast calls for a category 5 hurricane in your area, the correct response is to swiftly withdraw sufficient cash, stock up on food and water, board up the house, gas up the car and vacate the area before the hurricane hits. Likewise, the time to plan ahead for the imminent fulfillment of a Bible prophecy is NOW!

After Noah alerted his family about his NOW prophecy, which concerned the coming worldwide flood, he had to go to his local hardware store and purchase the necessary tools and construction materials to begin building his ark.

After Joseph interpreted Pharaoh's dream, which concentrated upon the NOW prophecy of seven years of plenty that would be followed by seven years of famine, he had to encourage all of the farmers of Egypt to expeditiously begin seeding and fertilizing their fields.

After Jeremiah issued his NOW prophecy, which warned that the Judeans would go into seventy years of Babylonian captivity, the Jews headed to their local Army Navy surplus stores to pick up their camping and survival gear.

NOW is the time for Iranians, Syrians, Israelis, Jordanians, Egyptians, Americans and the rest of the mankind to acquire the necessary goods and materials that they will specifically need to prepare for the fulfillment of the ancient prophecies that will directly affect them!

End-Time's Christian Survival

Since these powerful NOW prophecies are forthcoming, it's prudent to prepare for them well in advance. There is biblical precedent for prophetic preparedness. It's smart to fill the storehouses with food in advance of a pending famine—that's what Joseph did in the Genesis 41 historic account. Joseph possessed invaluable prophetic insights into the near future, and he promptly took the necessary measures to provide for the Egyptians.

In the process, his Hebrew posterity was also preserved. The predicted famine that plagued Egypt also struck the land of Canaan. Canaan was where Joseph's immediate family members resided. The famine forced Joseph's family to seek exile into Egypt. Due to the preparedness of the Egyptians, these chosen Hebrew peoples survived their severe famine. This historical account is recorded in Genesis 42-47. One of the most memorable quotes that characterized this incredible story is when Joseph said to his brothers,

> "Do not be afraid, for *am* I in the place of God? But as for you, you meant evil against me; *but* God meant it for good, in order to bring it about as *it is* this day, to save many people alive. Now therefore, do not be afraid; I will provide for you and your little ones." And he comforted them and spoke kindly to them."
>
> — Genesis 50:19-21

Joseph's actions were blessed, because they glorified God, and were in alignment with the Lord's plan for that time. Joseph asks his brothers, "*Am I in the place of God?*" The answer spiritually was yes, but geographically Egypt wasn't the place that God called home. The land of Canaan was part of the Promised Land given to Abraham in Genesis 15:18, whereas most of Egypt was not. Joseph's rhetorical question illustrates that *the place of God*, Who is omnipresent, is wherever the Lord's presence is. In this case, Joseph was blessed for his faith in God, by the presence of God.

Joseph experienced severe hardships in his life, but he never lost faith in his God. He knew that the Lord was in charge and worked all things together for the good according to His purposes. Romans 8:28 says, "*And we know that all things work together for good to those who love God, to those who are the called according to His purpose.*" Even the famine crisis in Egypt and Canaan worked together for the good of Joseph's family, who were "*called according to*" God's purposes.

The NOW prophecies will adversely affect the peoples and places that feel the full brunt of the blow. However, the Lord will be faithful to make all things work together for the good of His affected followers, *to those who are the called according to His purpose.*

Preparing Mentally for the NOW Prophecies

I recently heard a quote on the Understanding the Times radio show hosted by Jan Markell, which encapsulates the importance of trusting in God to make all circumstances work out favorably for the believer. The quote came from holocaust survivor Anita Dittman, who co-authored the book with Jan Markell entitled, "*Trapped in Hitler's Hell.*"

Anita was headed for extermination in the Auschwitz concentration camp, but before she was scheduled to depart, she was able to attend a local church for a Christmas service. Anita thought it might be her last Christmas. Anita, a believing Jew, said something like this, "*Safety in any situation is not the absence of danger, but rather it is the presence of God in that circumstance.*"[60]

Anita Dittman is still alive today and her faith in God is inspirational. If a Christian exemplifies the immovable faith of an Anita Dittman and follows the lessons of Joseph by preparing for prophetic events, his or her actions can preserve the posterity of their family, and also serve as a testimony to an unbelieving spectator. The goal is to temper the survival efforts with a clear demonstration of whole-hearted faith in Christ, and a wholesome understanding of Bible prophecy. This mentality will enable the believer to remain spiritually and emotionally stable and simultaneously be a good witness throughout the fulfillment of the NOW prophecies.

The believer's behavior should resemble that of Noah's. While his ark was being constructed, he used the opportunity to preach to those curious about his foreknowledge of the flood. Although only his immediate family heeded his warnings, the inaction of those in denial did not deter him from taking the necessary survival measures. In the process, his posterity was also preserved.

Noah's actions were also blessed because they glorified God, and were in alignment with the Lord's plan for that time. Additionally, stockpiling some cash, gas, and goods in advance of the fulfillment of a Bible prophecy can insulate the believer from the predictable panic and hysteria that could follow. Long gas lines, food shortages, and inaccessible ATM machines for instance, can be temporarily avoided. This buys time for the potential of some resemblance of normalcy to resume in the affected area. In the process, the believer can keep his full focus upon God and his posterity can also be preserved.

The Importance of Bible Prophecy

Before explaining the multi-layered approach of preparing physically for a NOW prophecy, I need to explain the importance of the NOW prophecy. All Bible prophecies, whether they are PAST, NOW, NEXT or LAST prophecies, are intended to accomplish a four-fold purpose. They are to,

- *Authenticate the sovereignty of God,*
- *Equip the followers of God for the days in which they live,*
- *Spare lives,*
- *Save souls.*

Authenticate the sovereignty of God – Isaiah 46:9-10 declares that only God can predict the future with 100% accuracy. The Lord's ability to declare the end from the beginning is one of His signature trademarks that sets Him apart from all of the false gods. When an ancient biblical prediction finds a future fulfillment, the Lord can justifiably say, *"I told you so in advance."* As impressive as this is, the Lord is not interested in merely impressing us, but rather He wants to inform us of what's forthcoming.

Equip the followers of God for the days in which they live – The Lord wants to inform us of the future because He wants to equip us for the pitfalls that await us. To equip someone is to prepare them for a particular activity or problem. It also means to provide them with necessary materials or supplies that they need to deal with that activity or problem.[61] The Lord wants to equip us so that we can survive the epic NOW event when it comes.

Spare lives – God wishes that none would perish, but that all would have abundant life on the earth and eternal life afterward. This is why John 3:16 explains that God sent Jesus, His only begotten Son, to die for our sins so that through faith in Him we could have eternal life. Ezekiel 33:11 says, *"I (God) have no pleasure in the death of the wicked, but* (desire) *that the wicked turn from his way and live."* Almost one-third of the Bible is devoted to prophecy, which evidences how important prophecy is to God. It should also be important to all of mankind because it is issued for everyone's benefit. In the examples of Noah, Joseph and Jeremiah listed above, Bible prophecy saved their lives and the lives of all those who, like them, prepared ahead to survive the calamity.

Save souls – The fact that the Lord shares, rather than keeps secret, His foreknowledge of the future through biblical prophecies, can make someone grow fond of Him. I did! I became a born again believer through learning about Bible prophecies. This happened while I was attending a Bible study on the book of Revelation that was taught by Dr. Chuck Missler. Revelation 19:10 says, "*Worship God! For the testimony of Jesus is the spirit of prophecy.*" Bible prophecy can and has lead people to the Lord because it testifies of Jesus Christ! It should not be shunned, which is sadly the case within so many churches today, but rather it should be preached alongside the gospel as a witnessing tool.

> "All Scripture (*including the Bible prophecies*) *is* given by inspiration of God, and *is* profitable for doctrine, for reproof, for correction, for instruction in righteousness, that the man of God may be complete, thoroughly equipped for every good work."
>
> — 2 Timothy 3:16-17; *emphasis added*

The Lord is not someone with too much time on His hands; He holds all time in His hands. God does not give us prophecy to impress us, but rather to inform us. This is because He loves us. Joseph said in Genesis 50:20, which was quoted above, "*God meant it for good, in order to bring it about as it is this day, to save many people alive.*" What was it that *saved many people alive*? It was the NOW prophecy that seven years of plenty would be swallowed up by seven years of famine in Egypt. Many people survived the seven severe years of famine because they were prepared in advance.

When the Lord issued the NOW prophecies centuries ago, He was not trying to SHOW OFF, but rather He was letting us know that He intends to SHOW UP! God will be with us to comfort and protect us when each NOW prophecy finds fulfillment. Like Anita Dittman says, "*Safety is not the absence of danger, but the presence of God.*"

The Three Facets of Bible Prophecy Awareness

There are three facets to learn about in order to achieve a full awareness of the role of Bible prophecy as purposed by God. They are; *the Prediction, the Preparation, and the Preservation.*

Stage One – the Prediction

When someone first becomes interested in Bible prophecy, the plethora of ancient predictions fascinates them. They marvel at the reality that the future can be known. They witness current world events begin to align with the details of the predicted event. It is a precious discovery, but one that comes with great responsibility. This is because people are prone to make major life changes in accordance with what they think the future holds. Noah, Joseph, Jeremiah and many other biblical figures attest to this. These peoples of the past wisely made major life changes in accordance with their specific NOW prophecies.

Let me share a personal story along these lines. While traveling on a plane to one of my first Bible prophecy conferences as a Christian author, I encountered a complete stranger who was reading a Christian book. He was seated directly across the aisle from me, so I struck up a lengthy, friendly conversation with him during the flight. He is a very private person, so the names and details of this testimony are purposely vague. He will be called Joe in this true life story.

I quickly realized that Joe was no stranger when it came to Bible prophecy. He knew his way around the entire Bible, especially the prophecies. Joe became very interested in the Psalm 83 prophecy that I shared with him because he was unfamiliar with this particular ancient prediction. Psalm 83 is the main theme of my first book called, *Isralestine, The Ancient Blue prints of the Future Middle East. Isralestine* came out in the summer of 2008, and our conversation took place in December of that same year. Before we deplaned to our differing destinations, I handed him an *Isralestine* book. It was a simple gift with no strings attached and I didn't know if he would read it, or if we would ever meet again.

About two months later, I received a phone call, from guess who? It was Joe, and he wanted to meet with me as soon as possible. Humbly I obliged, and so we met over lunch the next day. During our luncheon, Joe proceeded to inform me that he owned a multi-million dollar international business that he had decided to sell after reading *Isralestine*. One of Joe's primary reasons for deciding to sell his business was because he didn't want to own his business when Psalm 83 found fulfillment. Joe expressed to me that he was nearing retirement and someday intended to sell his business anyway, but his concerns about Psalm 83 motivated him to sell now.

Joe, like me, had come to the similar conclusion that Psalm 83 could occur in the near future, and that upon its fulfillment, life in the Middle East and America would be dramatically different. Hearing about Joe's major life decision to sell his long established business was a WOW moment for me! It was a real wakeup call, because I was spiritually hanging out in the first facet of fascination with Bible prophecy at the time. This experience made me take the responsibilities of my new ministerial calling deeper to heart. There's a whole lot more to our story, but the short version is that Joe sold his business shortly thereafter

The example of Joe illustrates how Bible prophecy can motivate someone to make a major business move based upon their understanding of a biblical prediction. For Joe, the move has so far turned out positive. However, on the flip side, there are dangers to be concerned about when Bible prophecies are misinterpreted. One example is in the case of radio evangelist Harold Camping. Below is a quote from Wikipedia about his story.

"Camping predicted that Jesus Christ would return to Earth on May 21, 2011, whereupon the saved would be taken up to heaven in the rapture, and that there would fol-

low five months of fire, brimstone and plagues on Earth, with millions of people dying each day, culminating on October 21, 2011, with the final destruction of the world."[62]

Needless to say, Camping's predictions were grossly inaccurate, went against what the bible directly says, and they were blatantly dangerous. Many people trusted in Camping's predictions and made major life changes in advance of May 21, 2011. Imagine if Joe, in the story above, would have sold his business based upon Harold Camping's deluded misinformation. Joe would not be a happy camper today!

The lesson to be learned in the prediction stage of Bible prophecy is that it comes with great accountability. Bible prophecy is not intended to be someone's mere reading entertainment or socialite table talk. It is a gift from God that requires the recipient to study it seriously. Proverbs 25:2 says, *"It is the glory of God to conceal a matter, But the glory of kings is to search out a matter."* Once the student of Bible prophecy realizes this, then they can graduate on to the second stage of understanding.

Stage Two – the Preparation

You don't have to look much past what's presently taking place in the Syrian revolution, the Palestinian – Israeli conflict, the re-emergence of post-cold war Russia or the dangerous Iranian nuclear scenario to become aware of stage two.

Christians are being beheaded and raped by ISIS. Israelis are being shot at by Hamas missiles and stabbed by Palestinians. Crimeans and Ukrainians are living under the stress and threats of Russian domination. Iranian Christians are being repressed by Iran's ruthless Islamic regime. All of the above have potential prophetic implications because Syria, Israel, Russia and Iran are all the subjects of unfulfilled Bible prophecies.

The point of stage two is that a biblical prediction will eventually transfer from the parchment to the pavement. Although the prophecies were once upon a time penned on paper, they were never intended to remain dormant there indefinitely. The foretelling was meant to find a future fulfillment and when it does, real people are going to be severely impacted.

The subject populations and places specified in the details of the prediction are going to get hit with the powerful punch of the prophecy. There will be suffering, just like there was at the time of Noah, Jeremiah and the others affected by the past biblical prophecies.

In the book of Revelation, the apostle John is instructed to take a little book from an angel. John followed his instructions and took the book.

> "So I went to the angel and said to him, "Give me the little book." And he said to me, "Take and eat it; and it will make your stomach bitter, but it will be as sweet as honey in your mouth." Then I took the little book out of the angel's hand and ate it, and it was as sweet as honey in my mouth. But when I had eaten it, my stomach became bitter."
>
> — Revelation 10:9-10

This is an illustration of stage two in Bible prophecy awareness. Stage one is fascinating. Learning about the future tastes sweet as honey. However, when you see real people suffering as the prophecy unfolds and nears its fulfillment; your belly becomes bitter with indigestion. A true Bible believing, loving Christian does not want to see anyone suffer. Even Jesus instructed His disciples to love their enemies in Matthew 5:44 and Luke 6:27, 35.

The Preparation stage is when the predictions are looked at in light of their realistic applications. The onlooker realizes the stage is set for the fulfillment of the foretelling. They can almost taste it. It was super sweet to chat about, but now it's time to get ready for the bitter blow. As the prophecies draw near, the time for entertaining chatter ends, and then it becomes time to sound the alarm! When it comes to the NOW prophecies, the time to simply teach about them is over. NOW it's time to prepare yourselves and other people for them!

Stage Three – the Preservation

It was stated earlier that the Lord intends to SHOW UP in the NOW prophecies. In places like Iran, the Syrian refugee camps and other repressed parts of the world, He already is! The chapter called, "The Nuclear NOW Prophecy of Iran," pointed out that Iranians are experiencing the Lord's presence through dreams, visions and personal encounters. This is also happening within the Syrian refugee camps.

The Lord knew that in the end times, places like these would be mostly shut off to Christian missionaries. This is why He has rolled up His sleeves and personally delivered upon His promises through the supernatural methods described in the book of Joel.

> "And it shall come to pass afterward That I will pour out My Spirit on all flesh; Your sons and your daughters shall prophesy, Your old men shall dream dreams, Your young men shall see visions. And also on My menservants and on My maidservants I will pour out My Spirit in those days.

> — Joel 2:28-29

The point of the third stage of preservation is that the Lord participates in the prophecy. The affected peoples don't go it alone. The Lord arrives in advance of the event, as is the case in Iran and Syria today. Moreover, He shows up within the episode, in order to comfort those affected by it. Lastly, He sticks around long after the epic event to receive the destitute that might cry out to Him in the aftermath.

Preparing Physically for the NOW Prophecies

Thus far, this chapter has demonstrated how biblical prophecy is intended to play an active role in present day Christianity. It is useful to prepare for the future and to evangelize the unsaved in the present. The attitude adopted by some Christians that, "*I will believe it when I see it fulfilled*," does a disservice to the Lord's four-fold purposes of Bible prophecy presented earlier. Don't wait to see if a NOW prophecy will happen, plan ahead in case it does!

The Multi Layers of Physical Preparation

There are different ways to plan ahead for an event, and they may vary depending on the nature of the event. In the case of the imminent destruction of Damascus in Isaiah 17:1, it's about departing from the city rather than stockpiling and hunkering down within the city. This is also the case in western Iran around the Bushehr province of the territory of ancient Elam. Jeremiah 49:36-37 clearly states that this area will experience a disaster that will force the evacuation of the affected peoples. In both instances, the chances of surviving these NOW prophecies by going through them are very slim.

Mansour, who was mentioned earlier in this book, and I have conversed about this matter pertinent to Iran. As a leader of Iran's underground church, he feels a burden to warn the Iranian Christians living in western Iran about the impending disaster described in Jeremiah 49:34-39. Mansour has shared with me that many of these Iranians are extremely impoverished and lack the financial means to move out of the area. As such, we have discussed a layered strategy for those unable to leave in advance of the disaster.

One idea for them is to bug out of the area at the first hints of war, before the prophecy finds fulfillment. The Jeremiah 49 prophecy of Elam could happen overnight like the destruction of Damascus in Isaiah 17:14, but it doesn't specify this. What it does inform is that the disaster in Iran could be of a nuclear nature. This means that the affected people will need to go quickly in the opposite direction of the potential nuclear fallout.

Providing time permits, there are at least three reasons that these Iranians should head to the east. First, the fallout will likely blow to the west toward the GCC Arab states on the other side of the gulf because of the prevailing winds in the area. Second, the Zagros Mountains will serve as a geographical barrier preventing the fallout from going to the east. Third, because to the east is ancient Persia, which is not directly involved in the Jeremiah prophecy of Elam. Persia survives beyond the Elam disaster to participate in Ezekiel 38:5, which appears to be a subsequent prophecy concerning Iran.

I have had a similar conversation with a friend of mine named Lisa, who lives in northern Israel. Lisa is concerned that the next Israel – Hezbollah war, which could be prophetic, will force northern Israelis into bomb shelters for prolonged periods of time. This happened in the war with Hezbollah in the summer of 2006. At that time, Hezbollah lobbed 4000 missiles over 34 days into Israel. On average, this was about 118 per day. Presently, Hezbollah is estimated to have 150,000 missiles and some military analysts predict that they will launch 1500 missiles per day in the next war.

Lisa doesn't want to leave presently or move permanently, but she does have plans to go stay with friends in Jerusalem on a moment's notice. On, or shortly before, day one of the next Hezbollah war, she will be attempting to flee to Jerusalem. Although Jerusalem could also come under attack, the odds are that it won't. This is because Jerusalem is the third holiest city in Islam, which might prevent Hezbollah from bombarding the city with missiles.

I provide these examples about Iran and Israel to demonstrate how people can plan ahead strategically, by thinking logically about the details of the relevant prophecy. In the case of America, the same principle applies. For example, every American should maintain an active Passport in the event they decide or need to leave the country. These are relatively inexpensive and easy to acquire. Every family member should have one.

A few other wise things to consider are listed below.

- Keep cash on hand in case the banks and ATM machines shut down. The cash should be broken down into small and large denominations. In a crisis, you don't want to buy a loaf of bread for $100 because the cashier ran out of change. Or, on the other end of the spectrum you don't want to buy a $1000 generator with a 1000 $1 bills.

- Always keep a bug out bag on hand that contains emergency items that enable you to survive for a few days until you can make other longer term preparations.

- Keep the gas tanks full at all times. If terrorist launch a dirty bomb or unleash a deadly virus in your town, you will need to evacuate quickly to a safer, out of the area location.

- Always keep a decent supply of non-perishable food and water stocked up.

- Don't forget the Bible, flashlights, matches, Swiss army knife, soap, band aids and toilet paper.

It is not the intent of this chapter to provide an extensive laundry list of ideas on how to survive a crisis. There are many guides and resources available over the Internet that are specifically designed for survival purposes. I advise that you research what survival resources work best for your budget and family needs.

Many households are only nine meals away from anarchy. This means that on average most families only have about a three day supply of food and water. By day four, the trip to the local supermarket would prove to be unfruitful, and probably very dangerous. Due to looting and stockpiling of the items people need to survive, supplies will be scarce.

The goal is to be prepared to endure whatever storm confronts you and your family. It doesn't matter whether it is a manmade crisis, natural disaster, or cosmic disturbance. There are precautionary measures that can be taken in advance. The fact that the fulfillment of a biblical prophecy could contribute to a crisis affecting you, should prompt you to get ready NOW.

Remember, if you are able to emulate Joseph's example in Egypt, be prepared to provide food, water and shelter for more people than just yourself. Although you may be prepared for a crisis, the odds are that some of your loved ones, friends and neighbors won't be. They will turn to you in their time of need. If your funds provide, double up on your survival needs. You and someone you love may someday be thankful that you, or another Christian brother and sister, did.

17

Preparing Spiritually For The NOW Prophecies

"In an acceptable time I have heard you, And in the day of salvation I have helped you." Behold, now *is* the accepted time; behold, now *is* the day of salvation.

— 2 Corinthians 6:2

Thus far, this book has purposed to prepare you mentally and physically for the fulfillment of the NOW prophecies. This chapter was reserved for the end in order to equip you spiritually. We are eternal beings that inhabit temporal bodies. We were created in the image of God, (Genesis 1:26), with a mind, body and a soul. Our triune existence operates harmoniously with God when we love Him with every fiber of our being. Jesus confirmed this with this exhortation;

"And you shall love the Lord your God with all your heart, with all your soul, with all your mind, and with all your strength.' This is the first commandment.'"

— Mark 12:30

The most important decision one can make in their entire lifetime is to receive Christ as their personal Lord and Savior. It is the sinner's passport to paradise! It's an all-inclusive package that provides a forgiven and changed life on earth now and a guaranteed future admission into heaven afterward.

Without God's forgiveness, the sinner cannot enter into heaven because earthly sin is not allowed to exist there. Otherwise, it would not be rightfully called "heaven." Jesus was sent into the world to provide a remedy for man's sin problem. The Bible teaches that we are all sinners and that the wages, (what we deserve), of sin is death, (spiritual separation from God forever). But God so loved us that He wanted to make a way so anyone could be forgiven and thus be allowed to enter heaven. God doesn't want anyone to perish, and has been patient with us so that we can turn from sin and find forgiveness, (by faith), in His son, Jesus.

> "For God so loved the world that He gave His only begotten Son, [*Jesus Christ*] that whoever believes in Him should not perish but have everlasting life.

> — John 3:16

> And this is eternal life, that they may know You, the only true God, and Jesus Christ [*Begotten Son of God*] whom You have sent."

> — John 17:1-3

These passages point out that people are perishing to the great displeasure of God, who loves them immeasurably. He wishes that none would perish, but that everyone would inhabit eternity with Him and His only begotten Son, Jesus Christ. Quintessential to eternal life is the knowledge of these two concepts.

Sin Separates Us from the Love of God

The apostle John reminds us in 1 John 4:8, 16 that God is love, but man lives in a condition of sin, which separates him from God's love. Romans 8:5-8 explains how sin manifests into carnal behavior that creates enmity between God and man.

"So then, those who are in the flesh cannot please God."

— Romans 8:8

The book of Romans instructs that sin entered into the world through Adam, and spread throughout all mankind thereafter. Additionally, Romans informs that sin is the root cause of death, but through Jesus Christ eternal life can be obtained.

"Therefore, just as through one man [*Adam*] sin entered the world, and death through sin, and thus death spread to all men, because all [*men*] sinned."

— Romans 5:12; *emphasis added*

"All we like sheep have gone astray; We [*mankind*] have turned, every one, to his own way; And the LORD has laid on Him [*Jesus Christ*] the iniquity of us all."

— Isaiah 53:6; *emphasis added*

"For the wages of sin *is* death, but the gift of God *is* eternal life in Christ Jesus our Lord."

— Romans 6:23

If this makes sense to you, and you:

1. Have humbled yourself to recognize that you are a sinner, living under the curse of sin, which has separated from your Creator.
2. Believe that Jesus Christ took your punishment for sin so that you could be pardoned, as the only way to be saved
3. Want to repent and start letting God make changes in your life to be in a right relationship with God,
4. And, want to do it right now,

Then you have come to the right place spiritually. It is the place where millions before you, and many of your contemporaries alongside you, have arrived.

Fortunately, you have only one final step to take to complete your eternal journey. This is because salvation is a gift of God. Christ paid the full price for all sin, past, present, and future, when He sacrificed His life in Jerusalem about 2000 years ago. Your pardon for sin is available to you through faith in the finished work of Jesus Christ, which was completed upon His bloodstained cross. His blood was shed on our behalves. He paid sins wages of death on our account.

You must now take the final leap of faith to obtain your eternal salvation. It is your faith in Christ that is important to God.

"But without faith *it is* impossible to please [*God*] *Him*, for he who comes to God must believe that He is, and *that* He is a rewarder of those who diligently seek Him."

— Hebrews 11:6; *emphasis added*

"In this you [*believer*] greatly rejoice, though now for a little while, if need be, you have been grieved by various trials, that *the genuineness of your faith, being much more precious than gold that perishes*, though it is tested by fire, may be found to praise, honor, and glory at the revelation of Jesus Christ, whom having not seen you love. Though now you do not see *Him,* yet believing, you rejoice with joy inexpressible and full of glory, receiving the end of your faith—the salvation of *your* souls."

— 1 Peter 1:6-9

Before the necessary step to salvation gets introduced it is important to realize and appreciate that salvation is a gift provided to us through God's grace. We didn't earn our salvation, but we must receive it. If you are one who has worked hard to earn everything you have achieved in life then you are to be commended. However, apart from living a sinless life, which is humanly impossible, there is nothing you as a sinner could have done to meet the righteous requirement to cohabitate in eternity with God. In the final analysis, when we see our Heavenly Father in His full glory, we will all be overwhelmingly grateful that Christ's sacrificial death bridged the chasm between our unrighteousness, and God's uncompromised holiness.

> "But God, who is rich in mercy, because of His great love with which He loved us, even when we were dead in [*sin*] trespasses, made us alive together with Christ (*by grace you have been saved*), and raised *us* up together, and made *us* sit together in the heavenly *places* in Christ Jesus, that in the ages to come He might show the exceeding riches of His grace in *His* kindness toward us in Christ Jesus. *For by grace you have been saved* through faith, and that not of yourselves; *it is the gift of God,* not of works, lest anyone should boast."

> — Ephesians 2:4-9; *emphasis added*

The Good News Gospel Truth

The term gospel is derived from the Old English "*god-spell,*" which has the common meaning "*good news,*" or "*glad tidings.*" In a nutshell, the gospel is the good news message of Jesus Christ. Jesus came because God so loved the world that He sent His Son to pay the penalty for our sins. That's part of the good news, but equally important is the "Resurrection."

This is the entire good news gospel;

> "For I delivered to you first of all that which I also received: that Christ died for our sins according to the

Scriptures, and that He was buried, and that He rose again the third day according to the Scriptures."

— 1 Corinthians 15:3-4

Christ resurrected which means He's alive and able to perform all of His abundant promises to believers. The Bible tells us that He is presently in heaven seated at the right hand side of God the Father waiting until His enemies become His footstool. Furthermore, from that position Christ also intercedes on the behalf of Christians. This intercession is an added spiritual benefit to you for becoming a believer.

"But this Man, [*Jesus Christ became a Man, to die a Man's death*] after He had offered one sacrifice for sins forever, sat down at the right hand of God, from that time waiting till His enemies are made His footstool. For by one offering He has perfected forever those who are being sanctified."

— Hebrews 10:12-14; *emphasis added*

"Who *is* he who condemns? *It is* Christ who died, and furthermore is also risen, who is even at the right hand of God, who also makes intercession for us."

— Romans 8:34

The resurrection of Christ overwhelmingly serves as His certificate of authenticity to all His teachings. He traveled through the door of death, and resurrected to validate His promises and professions. This can't be said of the claims of Buddha (Buddhism), Mohammed (Islam), Krishna (Hinduism), or any of the other host of deceased, human, non-resurrected, false teachers. All the erroneous teachings they deposited on the living side of death's door were invalidated when they died and lacked the power to conquer death itself, as Jesus has done.

One of Christ's most important claims is;

"Jesus said to him, "I am the way, the truth, and the life. No one comes to the [*heavenly*] Father except through Me.""

— John 14:6; *emphasis added*

This is a critical claim considering eternal life can only be obtained by knowing the heavenly Father, and Christ, whom He [the Father] sent, according to John 17, listed earlier in this chapter. Most importantly, the resurrection proves that death has an Achilles heel. It means that its grip can be loosed from us, but only by Christ who holds the power over death.

"O Death, where is your sting? O Hades, where is your victory?" The sting of death *is* sin, and the strength of sin *is* the law. But thanks *be* to God, who gives us the victory [*over Death and Hades*] through our Lord Jesus Christ."

— 1 Corinthian 15:55-57; *emphasis added*

How to be Saved – You Must Be Born Again

"Jesus answered and said to [*Nicodemus*] him, "Most assuredly, I say to you, unless one is born again, he cannot see the kingdom of God.""

— John 3:3; *emphasis added*

Jesus told Nicodemus, a religious leader of his day, that entrance into the kingdom of god required being born again. This is a physical impossibility, but a spiritual necessity, and why faith plays a critical role in your salvation. You can't physically witness your new birth; it is a spiritual accomplishment beyond your control that happens upon receiving Christ as your Lord and Savior. God takes full responsibility for your metamorphosis into a new creation at that point.

"Therefore, if anyone *is* in Christ, *he is* a new creation;
old things have passed away; behold, all things have
become new."

— 2 Corinthians 5:17

You must trust God to perform on His promise to escort you through the doors of death into eternity, and to process you into the likeness of Christ. This is the ultimate meaning of being born again, and alongside Christ, is a responsibility undertaken by the third member of the Trinity, the Holy Spirit. Christ holds the power over Death and Hades, but the Holy Spirit is your "*Helper*" that participates in your spiritual processing.

"I *am* He [*Jesus Christ*] who lives, and was dead, and
behold, I am alive forevermore. [*Resurrected*] Amen. And
I have the keys of Hades and of Death."

— Revelation 1:18; *emphasis added*

"If you love [*Christ*] Me, keep My commandments. And I
will pray the Father, and He will give you another Helper
[*Holy Spirit*], that He may abide with you forever— the
Spirit of truth, whom the world cannot receive, because it
neither sees Him nor knows Him; but you know Him, for
He dwells with you and will be in you."

— John 14:15-17; *emphasis added*

"These things I have spoken to you while being present with you. But the Helper, the Holy Spirit, whom
the Father will send in My name, He will teach you all
things, and bring to your remembrance all things that I
said to you."

— John 14:25-26

In order for you to successfully crossover from death to eternal life, *at the appointed time,* God has to work his unique miracle. Christ's resurrection demonstrated that He possesses the power to provide you with everlasting life. Death was not eliminated in the resurrection, it was conquered.

This is why the full gospel involves both God's love and power. His love for us would be of little benefit if it ended with our deaths. His love and power are equally important for our eternal assurance.

Therefore, we are informed in Romans 10, the following:

> "But what does it say? *"The word is near you, in your mouth and in your heart"* (that is, the word of faith which we preach): that if you confess with your mouth the Lord Jesus and believe in your heart that God has raised Him from the dead, you will be saved. For with the heart one believes unto righteousness, and with the mouth confession is made unto salvation. For the Scripture says, *"Whoever believes on Him will not be put to shame."* For there is no distinction between Jew and Greek, for the same Lord over all is rich to all who call upon Him. For *"whoever calls on the name of the Lord shall be saved."*"
>
> — Romans 10:8-13

These Romans passages sum it up for all who seek to be saved through Christ. We must confess that Jesus Christ is Lord, and believe in our hearts that God raised Him from the dead.

The Sinner's Prayer for Salvation

Knowing that confession of Christ as Lord, coupled with a sincere faith that God raised Him from the dead are salvation requirements, the next step is customarily to recite a sinner's prayer in order to officiate one's salvation.

Definition of the Sinner's Prayer

"A sinner's prayer is an evangelical term referring to any prayer of humble repentance spoken or read by individuals who feel convicted of the presence of sin in their life and desire to form or renew a personal relationship with God through his son Jesus Christ. It is not intended as liturgical like a creed or a confiteor. It is intended to be an act of initial conversion to Christianity, and also may be prayed as an act of recommitment for those who are already believers in the faith. The prayer can take on different forms. There is no formula of specific words considered essential, although it usually contains an admission of sin and a petition asking that the Divine (Jesus) enter into the person's life."[63]

Example of the Sinner's Prayer

Below is a sample Sinner's Prayer taken from the Salvation Prayer website. If you are ready to repent from your sins, and to receive Jesus Christ as your personal Lord and Savior, read this prayer will all sincerity of heart to God.

> *Dear God in heaven, I come to you in the name of Jesus. I acknowledge to You that I am a sinner, and I am sorry for my sins and the life that I have lived; I need your forgiveness.*

> *I believe that your only begotten Son Jesus Christ shed His precious blood on the cross at Calvary and died for my sins, and I am now willing to turn from my sin.*

> *You said in Your Holy Word, Romans 10:9 that if we confess the Lord as our God and believe in our hearts that God raised Jesus from the dead, we shall be saved.*

> *Right now I confess Jesus as the Lord of my soul.*

With my heart, I believe that God raised Jesus from the dead. This very moment I receive Jesus Christ as my own personal Savior and according to His Word, right now I am saved.

Thank you Jesus for your unlimited grace which has saved me from my sins. I thank you Jesus that your grace never leads to license for sin, but rather it always leads to repentance. Therefore Lord Jesus transform my life so that I may bring glory and honor to you alone and not to myself.

Thank you Jesus for dying for me and giving me eternal life.

Amen.[64]

Congratulations and welcome into the household of God!

Below are the congratulatory words and recommendations also taken from the Salvation Prayer website. If you just prayed the Sinner's Prayer please be sure to read this section for further guidance.

"If you just said this prayer and you meant it with all your heart, we believe that you just got saved and are born again. You may ask, "Now that I am saved, what's next?" First of all you need to get into a bible-based church, and study God's Word. Once you have found a church home, you will want to become water-baptized. By accepting Christ you are baptized in the spirit, but it is through water-baptism that you show your obedience to the Lord. Water baptism is a symbol of your salvation from the dead. You were dead but now you live, for the Lord Jesus Christ has redeemed you for a price! The price was His death on the cross. May God Bless You!"[65]

Remember, being born again is a spiritual phenomenon. You may have felt an emotional response to your commitment to Christ, but don't be concerned if fireworks didn't spark, bands didn't march, sirens didn't sound, or trumpets didn't blast in the background at the time. There will be plenty of ticker-tape for us in heaven, which is where our rewards will be revealed. If you believed and meant what you said, you can be assured God, Who sent His Son to be crucified on our behalf, heard your every word. Even the angels in heaven are rejoicing.

"Likewise, I say to you, there is joy in the presence of the angels of God over one sinner who repents."

— Luke 15:10; *emphasis added*

Welcome to the family...!

Appendices

Appendix 1

The Text of Psalm 83 and Ezekiel 38:1-39:20

The Text of Psalm 83:1-18

(New King James Version)

1. Do not keep silent, O God! Do not hold Your peace, And do not be still, O God!

2. For behold, Your enemies make a tumult; And those who hate You have lifted up their head.

3. They have taken crafty counsel against Your people, And consulted together against Your sheltered ones.

4. They have said, "Come, and let us cut them off from being a nation, That the name of Israel may be remembered no more."

5. For they have consulted together with one consent; They form a confederacy against You:

6. The tents of Edom [Palestinians refugees including West Bank Palestinians] and the Ishmaelites [Saudis]; Moab [central Jordanians] and the Hagrites [or Hagarenes— Egyptians];

7. Gebal [Lebanese], Ammon [northern Jordanians], and Amalek [Arabs of the Sinai area]; Philistia [Palestinians of the Gaza, including Hamas] with the inhabitants of Tyre [Lebanese, including Hezbollah];

8. Assyria [Syrians and northern Iraqis] also has joined with them; They have helped the children of Lot. Selah

9. Deal with them as with Midian, as with Sisera, as with Jabin at the Brook Kishon,

10. Who perished at En Dor, who became as refuse on the earth.

11. Make their nobles like Oreb and like Zeeb, Yes, all their princes like Zebah and Zalmunna,

12. Who said, "Let us take for ourselves The pastures of God [Promised Land] for a possession."

13. O my God, make them like the whirling dust, like the chaff before the wind!

14. As the fire burns the woods, and as the flame sets the mountains on fire,

15. So pursue them with Your tempest, and frighten them with Your storm.

16. Fill their faces with shame, that they may seek Your name, O LORD.

17. Let them be confounded and dismayed forever; Yes, let them be put to shame and perish,

18. That they may know that You, whose name alone is the LORD, are the Most High over all the earth.

The Text of Ezekiel 38:1-23

(New King James Version)

1. Now the word of the LORD came to me, saying,

2. Son of man, set your face against Gog, of the land of Magog, the prince of Rosh, Meshech, and Tubal, and prophesy against him,

3. and say, 'Thus says the Lord GOD: "Behold, I *am* against you, O Gog, the prince of Rosh, Meshech, and Tubal.

4. I will turn you around, put hooks into your jaws, and lead you out, with all your army, horses, and horsemen, all splendidly clothed, a great company *with* bucklers and shields, all of them handling swords.

5. Persia, Ethiopia, and Libya are with them, all of them *with* shield and helmet;

6. Gomer and all its troops; the house of Togarmah *from* the far north and all its troops—many people *are* with you.

7. "Prepare yourself and be ready, you and all your companies that are gathered about you; and be a guard for them.

8. After many days you will be visited. In the latter years you will come into the land of those brought back from the sword *and* gathered from many people on the mountains of Israel, which had long been desolate; they were brought out of the nations, and now all of them dwell safely.

9. You will ascend, coming like a storm, covering the land like a cloud, you and all your troops and many peoples with you."

10. 'Thus says the Lord GOD: "On that day it shall come to pass *that* thoughts will arise in your mind, and you will make an evil plan:

11. You will say, 'I will go up against a land of unwalled villages; I will go to a peaceful people, who dwell safely, all of them dwelling without walls, and having neither bars nor gates'—

12. to take plunder and to take booty, to stretch out your hand against the waste places *that are again* inhabited, and against a people gathered from the nations, who have acquired livestock and goods, who dwell in the midst of the land.

13. Sheba, Dedan, the merchants of Tarshish, and all their young lions will say to you, 'Have you come to take plunder? Have you gathered your army to take booty, to carry away silver and gold, to take away livestock and goods, to take great plunder?'"

14. "Therefore, son of man, prophesy and say to Gog, 'Thus says the Lord GOD: "On that day when My people Israel dwell safely, will you not know *it?*

15. Then you will come from your place out of the far north, you and many peoples with you, all of them riding on horses, a great company and a mighty army.

16. You will come up against My people Israel like a cloud, to cover the land. It will be in the latter days that I will bring you against My land, so that the nations may know Me, when I am hallowed in you, O Gog, before their eyes."

17. Thus says the Lord GOD: "Are *you* he of whom I have spoken in former days by My servants the prophets of Israel, who prophesied for years in those days that I would bring you against them?

18. "And it will come to pass at the same time, when Gog comes against the land of Israel," says the Lord GOD, "*that* My fury will show in My face.

19. For in My jealousy *and* in the fire of My wrath I have spoken: 'Surely in that day there shall be a great earthquake in the land of Israel,

20. so that the fish of the sea, the birds of the heavens, the beasts of the field, all creeping things that creep on the earth, and all men who *are* on the face of the earth shall shake at My presence. The mountains shall be thrown down, the steep places shall fall, and every wall shall fall to the ground.'

21. I will call for a sword against Gog throughout all My mountains," says the Lord GOD. "Every man's sword will be against his brother.

22. And I will bring him to judgment with pestilence and bloodshed; I will rain down on him, on his troops, and on the many peoples who *are* with him, flooding rain, great hailstones, fire, and brimstone.

23. Thus I will magnify Myself and sanctify Myself, and I will be known in the eyes of many nations. Then they shall know that I *am* the LORD.'"

The Text of Ezekiel 39:1-20

(New King James Version)

1. And you, son of man, prophesy against Gog, and say, 'Thus says the Lord GOD: "Behold, I *am* against you, O Gog, the prince of Rosh, Meshech, and Tubal;

2. and I will turn you around and lead you on, bringing you up from the far north, and bring you against the mountains of Israel.

3. Then I will knock the bow out of your left hand, and cause the arrows to fall out of your right hand.

4. You shall fall upon the mountains of Israel, you and all your troops and the peoples who *are* with you; I will give you to birds of prey of every sort and *to* the beasts of the field to be devoured.

5. You shall fall on the open field; for I have spoken," says the Lord GOD.

6. And I will send fire on Magog and on those who live in security in the coastlands. Then they shall know that I *am* the LORD.

7. So I will make My holy name known in the midst of My people Israel, and I will not *let them* profane My holy name anymore. Then the nations shall know that *I am* the LORD, the Holy One in Israel.

8. Surely it is coming, and it shall be done," says the Lord GOD. "This *is* the day of which I have spoken.

9. "Then those who dwell in the cities of Israel will go out and set on fire and burn the weapons, both the shields and bucklers, the bows and arrows, the javelins and spears; and they will make fires with them for seven years.

10. They will not take wood from the field nor cut down *any* from the forests, because they will make fires with the weapons; and they will plunder those who plundered them, and pillage those who pillaged them," says the Lord GOD.

11. "It will come to pass in that day *that* I will give Gog a burial place there in Israel, the valley of those who pass by east of the sea; and it will obstruct travelers, because there they will bury Gog and all his multitude. Therefore they will call *it* the Valley of Hamon Gog.

12. For seven months the house of Israel will be burying them, in order to cleanse the land.

13. Indeed all the people of the land will be burying, and they will gain renown for it on the day that I am glorified," says the Lord GOD.

14. "They will set apart men regularly employed, with the help of a search party, to pass through the land and bury those bodies remaining on the ground, in order to cleanse it. At the end of seven months they will make a search.

15. The search party will pass through the land; and *when anyone* sees a man's bone, he shall set up a marker by it, till the buriers have buried it in the Valley of Hamon Gog.

16. *The* name of *the* city *will* also *be* Hamonah. Thus they shall cleanse the land."'

17. "And as for you, son of man, thus says the Lord GOD, 'Speak to every sort of bird and to every beast of the field: "Assemble yourselves and come; Gather together from all sides to My sacrificial meal Which I am sacrificing for you, A great sacrificial meal on the mountains of Israel, That you may eat flesh and drink blood.

18. You shall eat the flesh of the mighty, Drink the blood of the princes of the earth, Of rams and lambs, Of goats and bulls, All of them fatlings of Bashan.

19. You shall eat fat till you are full, And drink blood till you are drunk, At My sacrificial meal Which I am sacrificing for you.

20. You shall be filled at My table With horses and riders, With mighty men And with all the men of war," says the Lord GOD.

Appendix: 2
Was Psalm 83 fulfilled in 1948?

Some people believe that the Psalm 83 prophetic war was fulfilled during the 1948 Arab-Israeli "War of Independence." The advocates for this view usually point to Psalm 83:1-8 to support their thesis. I disagree with this teaching for the reasons expressed in this Appendix.

Using the baseball idiom, "*Three strikes and you are out,*" the first strike against this thinking is found in the very first verse of Psalm 83, which reads; "*Do not keep silent, O God! Do not hold Your peace, And do not be still, O God!*" (Psalm 83:1; emphasis added)

Strike one, in 1948, the Lord kept very "*silent*" about this prophecy. In fact, the Lord kept fairly silent about Psalm 83 for about 3000 years until 2008, when I released my first book about this prophecy. The book is entitled, "*Isralestine, The Ancient Blueprints of the Future Middle East.*" This work addresses the prelude, episode and aftermath of the Psalm 83 prophecy. Prior to its release there was very little spoken or written about Psalm 83 as a Bible prophecy.

Psalm 83 did not find fulfillment in 1948 because the Lord kept silent at the time. Amos 3:7 says, "*Surely the Lord GOD does nothing, Unless He reveals His secret to His servants the prophets.*" With Amos 3:7 in mind, why did the Lord keep silent about Psalm 83 prior to 1948? The obvious answer would be because 1948 was not the fulfillment of Psalm 83.

Strike two, is found in verse 6 against a 1948 fulfillment, which reads; "*The tents of Edom and the Ishmaelites; Moab and the Hagrites.*" (Psalm 83:6). In the Bible the use of "*the tents of,*" often refers to a refugee scenario, like exiles encamped in tents.

Psalm 83:6 identifies the "*tents of Edom*" as a member of the Psalm 83 Arab confederacy. The Palestinians today have Edomite descendants within their ethnicity. Edomites, as it applies contextually in this verse, didn't become tent dwellers until after the war of 1948. This is when the Edomites became refugees. These refugees, referred to as the Palestinian refugees today, are the unplanned casualties that resulted from the 1948 war.

This is basically what happened at the time; in the early months of 1948, the Arab states warned their Arab counterparts living in Palestine to vacate the territory. The land was named Palestine at the time. However, on May 14, 1948, Palestine was renamed Israel as part of U.N. Resolution 181.

The Arab countries surrounding Israel refused to recognize this name change. They immediately waged war against Israel in order to destroy the Jewish state and preserve the name of Palestine. However, that was a terrible miscalculation because Israel won that war against all odds. As a result, the thousands of Arabs that left Palestine in advance of the war, found themselves without a homeland to return to in Israel after the war. Over six decades later, the Middle East is still seeking to resolve this refugee crisis.

Psalm 83 did not find fulfillment in 1948 because the *tents of Edom* didn't technically exist at the time. The *tents of Edom* became a reality after the war of 1948. Although nine of the members of the Psalm 83 confederacy assembled together in the 1948 war, the tenth member, the tents of Edom, was missing from that coalition.

Strike three, is found in the details of Psalm 83:9-18. These passages contain the petition of Asaph to empower the IDF like was done in Judges Chapters 4-8 with Gideon against the Midianites and Deborah and her general Barak against the Canaanites. The Midianites and Canaanites were soundly defeated, and as Judges 8:28 says, the Midianite oppression of the Israelites was over forever. This was also the case with the Canaanites upon their defeat. I have yet to find any biblical or historical evidence that either the Midianites or the Canaanites ever oppressed the Israelis subsequent to these defeats.

"Thus Midian was subdued before the children of Israel, so that they lifted their heads no more. And the country was quiet for forty years in the days of Gideon." Judges 8:28

The Arabs of Psalm 83 today still don't recognize Israel's right to exist and still oppress Israel. Psalm 83:9-18 are descriptive verses that call for the total end of the Psalm 83 confederate aggression. Since these Psalm 83 belligerents still oppress Israel, it is safe to presume that these relevant verses remain unfulfilled.

To finish the baseball analogy, the argument that Psalm 83 was fulfilled in 1948 strikes out because Psalm 83:9-18 has not happened yet. Psalm 83:18 says, "*That they may know that You, whose name alone is the LORD, Are the Most High over all the earth.*"

In this last verse the Psalmist expresses hope, that at the conclusion of the Psalm 83 war, the defeated Arab survivors will recognize the one true God of the Bible. Do the Palestinian refugees currently believe that Jehovah is the one true God? What about the Arabs states in Psalm 83 of Egypt, Syria, Iraq, Lebanon, Jordan, Saudi Arabia, do they believe in the God of the Bible. How about the terrorist populations of Hamas, Hezbollah, ISIS and the others possibly participating in Psalm 83, do they realize that Jehovah's *name alone is the LORD?* The answer to these three questions presently is NO, NO and NO. This implies that Psalm 83 hasn't happened yet, but it could occur NOW!

The Problems with Ezekiel 38:7-13 having been fulfilled in 1948

If Psalm 83 was fulfilled in 1948, then presumably Israel could presently be dwelling in the conditions described in Ezekiel 38:7-13. These verses foretell that Israel will be dwelling securely in the midst of the Promised Land without walls, bars or gates and that the nation will be extremely prosperous, because Israel's plunder and booty is what the Magog invaders are after. This is absolutely not the case today! Israel is the most fenced in and fortified nation in the world. There is no way that Israel is presently dwelling securely, and in my estimation, this is because Psalm 83 remains unfulfilled.

These are just a few of the reasons I still believe Psalm 83 remains unfulfilled, imminent and precedes the Ezekiel 38 and 39 prophecies. Also worth an honorable mention in this regard is the fact that some of the supporting countries of the 1948 war, like Pakistan and Sudan, do not appear to be part of the Psalm 83 Arab confederacy.

Appendix 3
Is Egypt in Psalm 83?

(Based on an article written by the author on 2/9/11. Linked at: http://prophecynewsstand.blogspot.com/2011/02/is-egypt-in-psalm-83.html)

Most modern-day equivalents of the Psalm 83:6-8 participants are easily identifiable today. Clearly, the territories of Edom, Moab, and Ammon represent modern-day Jordan. Furthermore, Tyre still exists in Lebanon and the Gaza Strip is located in ancient Philistia. However, Egypt is more difficult to identify, causing some scholars to question its existence in this Psalm. Among them is the respected broadcast journalist David Dolan. He authored a book in 2001 entitled *Israel in Crisis, What Lies Ahead.* Dolan's book, along with Dr. Arnold Fruchtenbaum's *Footsteps of the Messiah*, were among the first books published that addressed Psalm 83 as a future war between Israel and its bordering Arab enemies. Dolan excluded, but Fruchtenbaum included, Egypt in the Psalm 83 confederacy. David Dolan wrote the following.

"Will Egypt eventually break its peace treaty with Israel? I suspect that in the end, the American-funded and trained army will not allow this to take place. I noted in my latest book, *Israel in Crisis*, that Egypt is not listed in Psalm 83 as being among a host of regional Arab powers that will attempt to destroy Israel in the prophesied end days, while Jordan, Lebanon and Syria are mentioned, along with the Palestinians." David Dolan 2/7/11

As much as I respect Dolan's work, I respectfully disagree with his assessment on Egypt's non-participation in Psalm 83. Here is what the Psalm says:

"O God, keep not thou silence: Hold not thy peace, and be not still, O God. For, lo, thine *enemies* make a tumult; And they that hate thee have lifted up the head. Thy take crafty counsel against thy people, And consult together against thy hidden ones. They have said, Come, and let us cut them off from being a nation; That the name of Israel may be no more in remembrance. For they have consulted together with one consent; Against thee do they make a covenant: The tents of Edom and the Ishmaelites; Moab, and the Hagarenes; *Gebal*, and Ammon, and Amalek; *Philistia* with the inhabitants of *Tyre*: Assyria also is joined with them; They have helped the children of Lot. Selah!" Psalm 83:1-8, ASV; *emphasis added*

The Enemies vs. The Haters

Asaph seems to identify two distinct groups inside the ten-member confederacy. He says "thine *enemies* make a tumult; And they that hate thee have lifted up the head." *The New American Standard Version* translates; "*Your enemies make an uproar, And those who hate You have exalted themselves*."

Who are the *enemies* and *haters* of God listed inside the Psalm? I cover this extensively in my book, *Isralestine, The Ancient Blueprints of the Future Middle East* in the chapter called "Olam Ebah, The Ancient Arab Hatred of the Jews."

The Psalmist says the Lord has those who hate Him, but unlike the general carnal hatred characteristic of sinful humanity described in Romans 8:7, it is a deeply rooted hatred dating back almost 4,000 years. These haters listed by Asaph include the Egyptian matriarch Hagar, alongside the ancient patriarchs: Ishmael, Edom (Esau), Moab, Ammon, and Amalek. These all had familial relations with Abraham and histories of aggression against Abraham, Sarah, Isaac, Jacob, and their Hebrew descendants.

Hagar mothered Abraham's first son Ishmael. Esau was Abraham's grandson from Isaac. Moab and Ammon were the children of Abraham's nephew Lot. Lastly, Amalek was Abraham's great-great grandson through the line of Esau. Esau fathered the Edomites according to Genesis 36:1.

These individuals coveted the rich contents of the Abrahamic Covenant and entered into family feuds with the true Hebrew recipients of the covenantal promises. These individuals, along with their Hebrew counterparts, were the Benjamin Netanyahus, King Abdullahs, and Ayatollah Khameneis of their time; from their loins all the modern nations were formed.

These jealous "haters" incubated an enmity against the Lord that manifested throughout the region against the Israeli descendants of Abraham, Isaac, and Jacob. The Bible calls it an "ancient hatred," also translated as a "perpetual enmity." Ezekiel 35:5 tells us it was spawned by Esau.

The two Hebrew words used by Ezekiel are *olam ebah*, which when used together can be translated as, "a condition stemming back long ago in ancient times, perpetuated throughout time, manifesting into hostility with no apparent end in sight." As time progressed, the Hebrews staked their covenantal claims throughout the Middle East. These claims included:

- Our God is the only God and you shall have no others before Him, (Exodus 20:3)

- We will be a "great nation" above all others, (Genesis 12:2)

- Arabs must bless Hebrews or be cursed, (Genesis 12:3)

- You Arabs are trespassing on our Hebrew lands. (Genesis 15:18)

Suffice it to say the other four members of Psalm 83, *Gebal, Philistia, Tyre,* and *Assyria,* found it favorable to their religious, real estate, and cultural needs to resist these Hebrew claims and embrace the ancient hatred, well established throughout the region. Thus, these four populations probably represent the *your enemies* group in Psalm 83.

Hagar's jealous behavior toward Sarah is one of the reasons we can include her among the Psalm 83 haters. Considering Hagar was an Egyptian, according to Genesis 16:1, and she arranged an Egyptian bride for her son Ishmael in Genesis 21:21, we can likely conclude the Hagarenes represent Egypt in Psalm 83, through her and Ishmael's family tree. However, it's not quite that simple. Some Bible translations list Hagarites or Hagrites, rather than Hagarenes. This has caused many to believe Psalm 83 is describing another ethnicity than Egyptians. This is because the Hagrites or Hagarites show up in 1 Chronicles 5:10, 19-20 and elsewhere as a tribe dwelling approximately 300 miles northeast of Egypt, east of Gilead.

The Hebrew word used by the Psalmist to identify the Hagarenes was *Hagri.* Both the *Strong's Hebrew and Greek Dictionaries,* and the *New*

American Standard Hebrew and Greek Dictionaries suggest *Hagri* has a possible matronymic relationship to "Hagar," the Egyptian matriarch.

Additionally, listed below are other reputable quotes supporting the Psalm 83 Hagar - Egyptian connection:

Holman Bible Dictionary —

HAGARITE (Hag' ahr ite) Name of nomadic tribe whom the tribe of Reuben defeated east of the Jordan River (1 Chron 5:10, 19-20). Reuben won because they called on and trusted in God. The tribal name is apparently taken from Hagar, Sarah's maid and mother of Ishmael (Gen. 16).

International Standard Bible Encyclopedia—

Hagarenes / Hagarites / Hagrites

An Arab tribe, or confederation of tribes (1 Ch 5:10, 19, 20 the King James Version "Hagarites"; 1 Ch 27:31 the King James Version "Hagerite"; Ps 83:6 "Hagarenes"), against which the Reubenites fought in the days of Saul. In Gen. 25:12-18 are recorded the descendants, "generations," of Ishmael, "whom Hagar the Egyptian Sarah's handmaid, bare unto Abraham."

New Commentary on the Whole Bible: Old Testament—

Ps. 83:6-8 tabernacles—i.e., tents. Edom—Esau's descendants; they were located southeast of the Dead Sea and repeatedly attacked Israel (Psa. 137:7; Obadiah). Ishmaelites—descendants of Hagar and Abraham (Gen. 25:12ff.) as are the "Hagarenes."

Barnes, Notes on the Old Testament – Ps. 83:6-8—

And the Hagarenes—The Hagarenes were properly Arabs, so called from Hagar, the handmaid of Abraham, the mother of Ishmael. Gen. 16:1; 25:12. As connected with the Ishmaelites they would naturally join in this alliance.

Due to the differences between the Hagarenes and the Hagrites in some Bible translations of Psalm 83:6, I emailed my friend Dr. Arnold Fruchtenbaum of Ariel Ministries in 2008. Dr. Fruchtenbaum, a graduate of Dallas Theological Seminary, ranks among today's most respected eschatologists. I asked him how certain he was that Psalm 83 identified Egypt through the Hagarenes. His email response to me confirmed that he felt comfortable that Egypt is identified through the Hagarenes in Psalm 83.

Lastly, those who omit Egypt from Psalm 83 need to explain Egypt's apparent future confrontation with Israel in Isaiah 19:16-18. Isaiah 19:16

declares Egypt will someday greatly fear Israel. From Isaiah's time until now, this fear has only been in place since Israel's defeat of Egypt in the wars of 1948, 1967, and 1973. It is this fear that drove former Egyptian President Anwar Sadat to make peace with Israel in 1979.

Isaiah 19:17 states this fear evolves into a terror of Israel that overtakes all of Egypt. Isaiah 19:18 predicts this terror results in Egypt allowing Hebrew to be spoken in five Egyptian cities. One of these cities will be renamed the "City of Destruction." These three passages encourage the possibility that Egypt's participation in Psalm 83 provokes the wrath of the Israel Defense Forces against at least five Egyptian cities. In the aftermath of an IDF victory over Egypt, five cities promote Hebrew as the spoken language. This suggests Jews migrate into these five cities taking their language, religion and culture with them.

Some suggest Isaiah 19 deals with the Antichrist's invasion of Egypt, specified in Daniel 11:42-43. Although portions of Isaiah 19 may find partial association with Daniel 11:42-43, it is doubtful that Isaiah 19:16-18 finds any association with that event.

Why would the Antichrist take over five Egyptian cities and allow Hebrew to become the spoken language? It is commonly understood the Antichrist will be attempting Jewish genocide at the time. If this is the case, it would be contrary to his overall purposes to allow five cities in Egypt to promote the language of Hebrew.

For the above reasons I strongly believe that Egypt is identified in Psalm 83. Therefore, I believe Egypt will someday break its peace treaty with Israel and join the Psalm 83 confederacy.

(This appendix is also included in the book called, *"Psalm 83: Missing Prophecy Revealed, How Israel Becomes the Next Mideast Superpower."* That appendix contains the footnotes that are not included in this appendix).

Appendix 4
Old Testament Allusions to the Rapture

Comments by the author Bill Salus: Several Old Testament allusions to the Rapture exist and are helpful to argue for a Pre-Trib Rapture timing. Many eschatologists have used Old Testament models, like these below written by Christian author Jim Tetlow, to validate the Rapture and its Pre-Seventieth Week timing. Normally I author all the appendixes in my books, but in this unique instance I obtained permission from my good friend Jim Tetlow to use his excellent work previously performed on this subject. [66]

Perhaps some of the strongest arguments in favor of a Pre-Tribulation, Pre-Seventieth Week of Daniel Rapture are found in the Old Testament. In the Old Testament we see "a shadow of the good things to come, and not the very image of the things" (Hebrews 10:1). The Holy Spirit explains that these Old Testament types are preserved for our learning: "For whatever things were written before were written for our learning, that we through the patience and comfort of the Scriptures might have hope" (Romans 15:4).

> "Now all these things happened to them (Old Testament characters) as examples, and they were written for our admonition, upon whom the ends of the ages have come" 1 Corinthians 10:11

Bible students are well aware that there are numerous Old Testament types that foreshadow a New Testament fulfillment. A classic example is when Abraham took his son, his only son Isaac, whom he greatly loved, to the land of Moriah to offer him there as a sacrifice – concluding that God was able to raise him from the dead (Genesis 22; Hebrews 11:17-19). Abraham is a beautiful type of our heavenly Father, and Isaac, his beloved son, is a striking picture of Jesus, who willingly laid down His life on Mount Moriah 2,000 years later.

Though the Rapture was hidden in part from Old Testament believers, the types found throughout foreshadow a future Rapture when God removes His people prior to pouring out His wrath on a Christ-rejecting world. Let's now review some of these beautiful types that foreshadow the Rapture:

1. In Noah's day there were those who passed through the flood (Noah and his family in the ark); there were those who perished in the flood (the unbelieving world); and there was Enoch who was "translated" or "caught up" before the judgment of God was poured out. Enoch walked with God (Genesis 5:24) and pleased Him (Hebrews 11:5), just as Christians who abide in Christ please God (1 John 3:22). Interestingly, from the time God told Noah to enter the ark, until the time when the waters of the flood were on the earth, God granted seven more days for the world to repent (Gen. 7:1-10). Perhaps this is a foreshadow of the final seven-year period culminating in the final judgment (Rev. 19:11- 21).

2. In Lot's day, Lot and his family were "removed" before God rained down His judgment on Sodom and Gomorrah (Genesis 19). God did not just "preserve" them through His wrath, He removed them prior to judgment. Jesus said that just before His return it would be like the days of Noah (Luke 17:26) and like the days of Lot (Luke 17:28). Judgment in Sodom COULD NOT occur until Lot was removed (Genesis 19:22)!

Remarkably, "while [Lot] lingered, the [angels] took hold of his hand, his wife's hand, and the hands of his two daughters, the Lord being merciful to him, and they brought him out and set him outside the city… Hurry, escape there. For I cannot do anything until you arrive there (v. 16, 22). In other words, they were forcibly removed prior to judgment and judgment could not commence until they safely arrived in the new city!

3.   Joseph (a type of Christ in many ways) takes a gentile bride before the 7-year famine begins (Genesis 41:45). Notice in the account of Joseph that after he received his gentile bride, his brethren (the Israelites) and the entire world suffered a Seven year famine. (Genesis 41:54-57). During this time of famine many came to Joseph for food. Similarly, after Jesus receives His Bride, his brethren the Jews (and many in the world), will turn to the Lord Jesus for relief (Rev. 7). How fitting that the Great Tribulation is called the time of "the time of Jacob's trouble, but he shall be saved out of it" (Jeremiah 30:7). It is also referred to as "the time of the Gentiles" (Ezekiel 30:3) and many gentiles will also be saved out of it (Rev. 7). The famine is a type of the Tribulation (Amos 8:11), and Egypt is a picture of the world. This account strongly suggests that Jesus will get His bride before the 70th Week of Daniel – before the famine that will come upon the entire world.

4.   In Joshua chapter 2, Rahab trusts the Lord and befriends the Jewish spies. By faith Rahab puts a scarlet thread in her window (a symbol of Christ's blood) and she and her family are "brought out" of Jericho before the city is burned with fire (Joshua 6). Rahab is a prostitute (Heb. 11:31) and a Gentile woman (Joshua 2), yet she is found in the Messianic line (Matt. 1:5). Rahab is therefore a beautiful picture of the church (the bride of Christ). Though formerly a prostitute, Rahab, by faith, was made clean and delivered from God's wrath. Amazingly, in this account, we again see seven days of warning preceding judgment (God's gracious delay to encourage repentance). The armies of God marched around the city six days, and on the seventh day they marched around the city seven times, and then the city was finally destroyed (Joshua 6).

5.   In 1 Samuel 25:39-42, Abigail is informed that King David (foreshadowing King Jesus) wants to take her as his bride. She immediately responds and "rose is haste" with five of her damsels to "depart" and go to David for the marriage. Compare this with Matthew 25:1-13 where five wise virgins who truly had oil went forth to meet the Bridegroom (Jesus) away from their dwelling place (earth). Interestingly, the name Abigail means the Father's joy!

6.   The Song of Solomon is an amazing picture of Christ and His church (Ephesians 5:29- 32). In the Song of Solomon 2:8-13, the Bride (the church) hears the voice of her Beloved (Jesus) coming for her, then in verse 10 and 13, the Bridegroom speaks and calls His bride to "Rise up, my love, my fair one, and come away." This is a beautiful foreshadow of our marriage and honeymoon in heaven!

7. Isaiah 26:20-21 also gives us a possible picture of the Rapture preceding the Tribulation: "Come, my people, enter your chambers, and shut your doors behind you; hide yourself, as it were, for a little moment, until the indignation is past. For behold, the LORD comes out of His place to punish the inhabitants of the earth for their iniquity; the earth will also disclose her blood, and will no more cover her slain." Apparently, believers are tucked away in heaven before the Tribulation falls on the earth. This may also apply to the Jews who hide away in Petra during the Tribulation.

8. In Daniel chapter 3, King Nebuchadnezzar (a type of the Antichrist, cf. Rev. 13) demands that the entire population bow down to his image. Daniel's three friends (Jews) are preserved through the fiery tribulation, but Daniel is nowhere to be found. Daniel was "ruler over the whole province of Babylon, and chief administrator over all the wise men of Babylon" (Dan. 2:48), yet he is missing from the account. Why? Daniel was apparently away. Might he be a type of the Church?!

9. In Zephaniah 2:2-3 we read: "Before the decree bring forth, before the day pass as the chaff, before the fierce anger of the LORD come upon you, before the day of the LORD'S anger come upon you. Seek the LORD, all you meek of the earth, who have upheld His justice. Seek righteousness, seek humility. It may be that you will be hidden in the day of the LORD'S anger." Believers will be hidden in the day of the Lord's anger (cf. Isaiah 26:20-21). See also: Zephaniah 1:7.

10. Malachi chapter 3 deals with the Day of the Lord. Interestingly, Malachi 3:18 implies two comings: "Then shall ye (believers) return, and discern between the righteous and the wicked, between him that serveth God and him that serveth him not." It becomes clear when we read the entire context of Malachi 3 that believers shall return to the earth. In order to return and discern, believers must have first been caught away to heaven. Isaac and Rebekah, as well as Ruth and Boaz, also provide beautiful pictures of Christ taking a Gentile bride – one who counts the cost and leaves their own family – but is not required to suffer through great tribulation or famine. Other examples could be expounded on, but these should be sufficient to show that Christians will be removed before God's wrath is poured out and likely before the 70th Week of Daniel.

Concluding comment by Bill Salus; An additional example of the Rapture is regarded with Elijah, who was translated to heaven while being alive.

> "Then it happened, as they continued on and talked, that suddenly a chariot of fire *appeared* with horses of fire, and separated the two of them; and Elijah went up by a whirlwind into heaven. 2 Kings 2;11

Endnotes

1. I believe this saying, "Did man's mistake equal God's providence," may have originated with Corrie Ten Boom.

2. Definition of Zionism was taken from this website: https://www.jewish-virtuallibrary.org/jsource/Zionism/zionism.html

3. Statistics obtained on 10/22/15 at this website: http://www.operation-world.org/hidden/evangelical-growth

4. This quote was taken from the Internet on 1/28/14 at this Internet site: http://english.alarabiya.net/en/views/news/middle-east/2013/07/24/Iranian-radiation-a-threat-to-GCC-water-security-.html

5. This quote is taken from the Internet as of 1/28/14 at this site: http://www.futuredirections.org.au/publications/food-and-water-crises/28-global-food-and-water-crises-swa/1230-gcc-co-operates-on-critical-water-security-measure-in-response-to-fears-of-iranian-nuclear-radiation.html

6. Quote taken from the Al Jazeera article entitled, "Gulf States Try to Tackle Water woes." The article is posted on the web as of 11/5/15 at this website: http://www.aljazeera.com/indepth/features/2014/01/gulf-states-tackle-water-woes-20141226487523277.html

7. Hebrew word for "reduced" is razah and translations were taken from the New American Hebrew and Greek Dictionaries and Strong's Hebrew and Greek Dictionaries.

8. Iranians sentenced to 91 lashes for Pharrell 'Happy' video. This is a headline from an article on the website linked here: http://www.telegraph.co.uk/news/worldnews/middleeast/iran/11103542/Iranians-sentenced-to-91-lashes-for-Pharrell-Happy-video.html

9. Captive in Iran is published by Tyndale Momentum and is available through the website: www.captiveiniran.com

10. Hormoz Shariat's ministry website is: http://iranaliveministries.org/

11. Dr. Reagan's website is www.lamblion.com

12. Al Gist's website is http://www.maranathaevangelisticministries.com/

13. Reagan quote taken from the May-June, 2013 edition of the Lamplighter Magazine, page 2.

14. Reagan quote taken from his article entitled, "Our Out-of-Control Court." The article was published at this website link: http://www.lamblion.com/enewsletter1/new_enewsletter_template_150629.html

15. Hitchcock quote taken from page 94 of his book the *Late Great United States*.

16. Statement quoted from Wikipedia at this website: https://en.wikipedia.org/wiki/Pornography_in_the_United_States#cite_note-cbsnews2003-7

17. The Golden Age of Porn was in the 1970's according to this website: https://en.wikipedia.org/wiki/Golden_Age_of_Porn. This is the decade that some of the first popularized porn movies came out. Movies like, "Deep Throat" (1972), "The Devil in Mrs. Jones" (1973) and "Debbie Does Dallas" (1978).

18. As a Senator Barack Obama said in June of 2008, that ""We are no longer just a Christian nation but also a Jewish nation, a Muslim nation, and a Buddhist nation, and a Hindu nation, and a nation of nonbelievers" Confirm the quote at this website: http://www.factcheck.org/2008/08/obama-and-the-christian-nation-quote/

19. 2 Chronicles 7:14, NKJV

20. Jeremiah 7:16, 11:14, 14:11

21. Jeremiah 25:11-12, 29:10

22. Isaiah 46:9-10FFF

23. British Isle statement was taken from this website: https://en.wikipedia.org/wiki/British_Isles on 12/15/15.

24. Dr. Mark Hitchcock quote taken from this website: http://www.lamblion.us/2010/02/hitchcock-discusses-us-in-ezekiel-38-39.html on 12/15/15.

25. Dr. J. R. Church quote taken from page 220. The Guardian of the Grail book is in reprint and available for purchase at www.prophecyinthenews.com... Here is another related website link related to this quote. http://www.faculty.ucr.edu/~legneref/bronze/fellview.htm

26. Pastor Chuck Smith quote taken from C2000 Series on Ezekiel 36-39. This series is available through Calvary Chapel Costa Mesa.

27. Cornwall information taken from this website heraldofhope.org.au/wp-content/uploads/2013/12/Tarshish-Britain-or-Spain.pdf on 12/18/15

28. Comment taken from this website article: http://heraldofhope.org.au/wp-content/uploads/2013/12/Tarshish-Britain-or-Spain.pdf

29. Quote taken from Wikipedia website at this link: https://en.wikipedia.org/wiki/British_Empire on 12/16/15.

30. Website for the Tarshish-Britain or Spain article is heraldofhope.org.au/wp-content/uploads/2013/12/Tarshish-Britain-or-Spain.pdf

31. World army rankings taken from the Global Firepower website linked here: http://www.globalfirepower.com/countries-listing.asp

32. The Temple Institutes website is: http://www.templeinstitute.org/

33. List of nations and their relationship to Israel can be found on the Internet as of 5/7/14 at this website: http://en.wikipedia.org/wiki/International_recognition_of_Israel

34. Gas mask data taken from this website on 12/30/15, http://www.haaretz.com/israel-news/.premium-1.576757

35. Recommended times to reach bomb shelters in Israel were taken from this website: http://www.nbn.org.il/aliyahpedia/government-services/post-aliyah-guides/national-emergency-preparation/

36. Population statistics were taken from searching on this website: http://www.worldometers.info/world-population/population-by-country/

37. This was quoted on 10/23/15 on this website. https://now.mmedia.me/lb/en/nownews/lieberman_we_will_destroy_damascus_if_hezbollah_attacks_northern_israel_

38. Israel strikes near Damascus taken from website on 10/23/15 http://www.bbc.com/news/world-middle-east-30370670

39. Quote taken on 11/17/15 from this website: http://www.jpost.com/Middle-East/Syrian-media-reports-Israeli-airstrike-near-Damascus-airport-432733

40. Quote from Middle East Burning by Dr. Mark Hitchcock on page 176 of the chapter called, "Will Syria Be Destroyed Soon."

41. "Israel's newest submarine leaves Germany, bound for Haifa" article taken from this website: http://www.timesofisrael.com/israels-newest-sub-leaves-germany-bound-for-haifa/

42. Al Arabiya news headline taken from this website: http://english.alarabiya.net/en/perspective/analysis/2014/08/31/ISIS-appeal-presents-Jordan-with-new-test.html

43. Israel National News article was taken from this website: http://www.israelnationalnews.com/News/News.aspx/193488#.Vowyj5v4PIU

44. INN news headline was taken from this website: http://www.israelnationalnews.com/News/News.aspx/196132#.Vo1cOfkrLIW

45. Jerusalem Post article is at this website: http://www.jpost.com/Middle-East/Report-Israel-US-prepared-to-help-Jordan-fight-ISIS-360848

46. ISIS headline taken from this website: http://www.usnews.com/news/articles/2014/12/02/after-joining-isis-ansar-bayt-al-maqdis-expands-in-egypt.

47. Jordan demographics taken from this website: https://en.wikipedia.org/wiki/Demographics_of_Jordan

48. This ISIS article is at this website: http://www.prophecydepotministries.net/2014/isis-psalm-83/

49. World army rankings gathered on 12/19/14 at this website: http://www.globalfirepower.com/countries-listing.asp

50. Hebrew word translations taken from New American Standard Hebrew and Greek Dictionaries.

51. Holman Bible Dictionary says Isaiah's ministry was between 740-701 BC.

52. Army rankings accessed over the Internet on 1/7/15 at this website: http://www.globalfirepower.com/countries-listing.asp

53. Internet sources on 10/10/12 http://www.google.com/publicdata/explore?ds=d5bncppjof8f9_&met_y=sp_pop_totl&idim=country:SAU&dl=en&hl=en&q=population+of+saudi+arabia, and http://www.google.com/publicdata/explore?ds=d5bncppjof8f9_&met_y=sp_pop_totl&idim=country:SAU&dl=en&hl=en&q=population+of+saudi+arabia

54. Rapture Ready (www.raptureready.com), Rapture Forums (www.rapture-forums.com), and The Pre-Trib Research Center (www.pre-trib.org).

55. Rapture quote from Dr. Reagan taken from his ministry's Lamplighter magazine, the January 2016 edition.

56. Jim Tetlow's entire article about the Rapture can be read at this Internet site as of 8/15/2011, http://www.eternal-productions.org/PDFS/articles/Rapture.pdf

57. The Church as the Bride of Christ is identified in Matthew 25, Ephesians 5, and Revelation 21 and 22.

58. Chuck Missler article accessed over the Internet on 8/12/11 at: http://www.khouse.org/articles/2003/449/.

59. Greek word is "polus," and the translations came out of the *New American Standard Hebrew and Greek Dictionaries.*

60. Jan Markell's website is: https://www.olivetreeviews.org/

61. Equip is defined this way in the Merriam-Webster online dictionary at this web link: http://www.merriam-webster.com/dictionary/equip

62. Wikipedia quote on Harold Camping taken from this site: https://en.wikipedia.org/wiki/Harold_Camping

63. Sinner's Prayer quote taken from Wikipedia over the Internet on 8/13/11 at this link: http://en.wikipedia.org/wiki/Sinner's_prayer

64. Sinner's prayer example was copied from the Internet on 8/13/11 at this website link: http://www.salvationprayer.info/prayer.html (slight emphasis was added in this appendix)

65. Quote welcoming those who prayed the sinner's prayer into the family of God copied over the Internet on 8/13/11 at this link: http://www.salvationprayer.info/prayer.html

66. Jim Tetlow has gone to be with the Lord. Before he passed away, Jim graciously permitted this part of his transcript located on the web at http://www.eternal-productions.org/PDFS/articles/Rapture.pdf, to be included any of my books.

Psalm 83
The Missing Prophecy Revealed

An ancient prophecy written over 3000 years ago reveals that the Arab states and terrorist populations, which presently share common borders with Israel, will soon confederate in order to wipe Israel off of the map. These enemies of Israel are depicted on the red arrows upon the book cover image, and their mandate is clear:

> They have said, "Come, and let us cut them off from being a nation, That the name of Israel may be remembered no more." (Psalm 83:4).

Psalm 83 predicts a climactic, concluding Arab-Israeli war that has eluded the discernment of today's top Bible scholars, and yet, the Middle East stage appears to be set for the fulfillment of this prophecy. While many of today's top Bible experts are predicting that Russia, Iran, Turkey, Libya, and several other countries are going to invade Israel according a prophecy in Ezekiel 38, this timely book explains how Psalm 83 occurs prior. Discover how Israel defeats their ancient Arab enemies, and why Americans need to stand beside Israel in this coming war! Here are a few endorsements from the experts:

"Invaluable New Insights"

– Dr. David Reagan, the founder of Lamb and Lion
Ministries and host of Christ in Prophecy Television

"I wish I would have written it"

– Dr. David Hocking, the founder
of Hope for Today Ministries

"Groundbreaking"

– Dr. Thomas Horn, bestselling author
and founder of Raiders News Network.

Buy your copy of Psalm 83, the Missing Prophecy
Revealed at *http://www.prophecydepot.com*

Psalm 83: The Missing Prophecy Revealed, How Israel Becomes the Next Mideast Superpower

Table of Contents

Revelation Road
Hope Beyond the Horizon

You are invited on a one-of-a-kind reading experience. Enjoy a novel and biblical commentary at the same time. This unique book is designed with appeal for both fiction and non-fiction audiences. George Thompson believes his grandson Tyler lives in the final generation. Lovingly, he prepares the lad for the treacherous road ahead. All young Tyler wanted was a chance to join his sister at Eastside Middle School in the fall, but the Arab Spring led to an apocalyptic summer disrupting his plans. Middle East wars and nuclear terror in America quickly turned his world upside down. Join the Thompson's on their journey through the Bible prophecies of the end times, and discover how their gripping story uncovers the silver lining of hope against the backdrop of global gloom and doom. The commentary section explains how their story could soon become your reality!

America and the Coming Mideast Wars DVD

According to ancient Bible prophecies a series of Mideast wars are coming and America plays a vital part in these apocalyptic battles. Will the USA support Israel and be divinely blessed, or will America put the Jewish state into harm's way and come under divine judgment? America and the Coming Mideast Wars is a DVD that cuts to the biblical chase of what currently matters most in America and the Middle East.

"The Future for Israel, Iran, and the Arab States," is the first lesson, and it points out that Israel is the victor of a climactic concluding Arab-Israeli war predicted over 3000 years ago in Psalm 83. It also identifies the prophecies concerning the desolations of Egypt, Syria, Iran, and many other countries currently dominating the Mideast news.

"America's Role in the Coming Prophetic Wars," is the second teaching that explains America's crucial role in the Psalm 83 war, the Ezekiel 38 Magog invasion, and the Armageddon campaign of the Antichrist.

"The TV Interviews" are included as a bonus feature that provides the viewer with additional new insights about the future of America and the countries and terrorist populations of the Middle East.

Visit *http://www.prophecydepot.com*
to purchase these and other products.

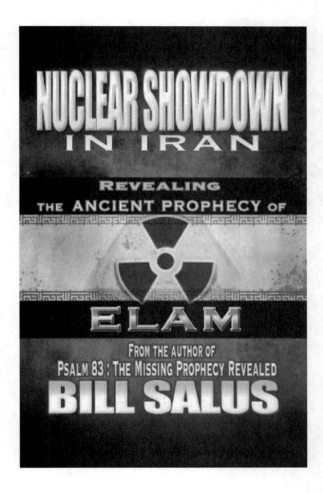

Missiles cloud Mideast skies over the Persian Gulf. Iran shuts down the Strait of Hormuz. Arab oil is choked off to world markets. Hezbollah and Hamas launch scores of missiles into Israel. Terror cells initiate cycles of violence in America. Global economies begin to collapse. Radioactivity permeates the skies over Bushehr's nuclear reactor. Countless Iranian's hastily seek refuge into neighboring nations. The Arabian Gulf becomes a cesspool of contamination. Desalinization plants can't process the polluted waters. A humanitarian crisis burgeons out of control. A disaster of epic biblical proportion has finally arrived in the Middle East!

About 2600 years ago the Hebrew prophets Jeremiah and Ezekiel issued parallel end times prophecies concerning modern-day Iran.

Today the rogue country is becoming a nuclear nation and aggressively advancing its hegemony throughout the greater Middle East. Nuclear Showdown in Iran, Revealing the Ancient Prophecy of Elam is a non-fiction thriller taking the reader on a journey of discovery through the eyes of the prophets and the minds of today's key national players.

Can anything good come from the evil that is about to befall us?

The ancient prophecy of Elam will reveal what God has ordained, what the prophets saw and what you need to know and do now.